Heckling Hitler
Caricatures of the Third Reich

Tina Yarborough

Chicago, 1989

Heckling Hitler

Caricatures of the Third Reich

Zbyněk Zeman

University Press of New England

Hanover and London, 1987

For Sophie

University Press of New England
Brandeis University
Brown University
Clark University
University of Connecticut
Dartmouth College
University of New Hampshire
University of Rhode Island
Tufts University
University of Vermont

Printed in Yugoslavia

Library of Congress Cataloging-in-Publication Data

Zeman, Zbyněk.
    Heckling Hitler.

    Bibliography: p.
    Includes index.
        1. Germany—Politics and government—1933-1945—
Caricatures and cartoons.   2. Hitler, Adolf, 1889-1945—
Caricatures and cartoons.   3. Wit and humor, Pictorial.
I. Title.
DD256.5.Z39   1987   943.086   86-40392
ISBN 0-87451-396-0
ISBN 0-87451-403-7 (pbk.)

Facing title-page: *'Burning Up!'*, Philip Zec, *Daily Mirror*
1940

Half title: *Now Let the Degenerate Democracies Show*,
Josef Čapek, *A Dictator's Boots*

Contents

Introduction 7

Young Hitler: The Making of a Famous Monster 17

The Nazi Movement 27

The Destruction of the Weimar Republic 41

The Leaders of the New Germany 55

The Thousand Year Reich 67

Matters of War and Peace 83

War: The Ultimate Goal 103

Notes 124

Index 125

Acknowledgments 128

Grim Reaper, Georges, *The Nation*, 5 April 1933

Introduction

The art of humorous invective directed at a country's rulers and mocking the social conditions for which they were held responsible flourished *par excellence* in England during the eighteenth, and in France during the nineteenth, century. Here and elsewhere it has usually thrived best in periods of sharp social conflict or high political tension, where rulers were self-confident enough to give artists a licence to mock them. Cartoonists, of course, have been able to direct their shafts across frontiers at targets which could do them no harm: Cranach's assaults on the Pope during the Reformation introduced that genre. But most caricature in Europe has grown out of the rich texture of local social life and politics; and it was easily accessible and understandable to a broad public, especially after the invention of printing in the fifteenth century.

Caricature derived from an ancient tradition. On the papyri from the time of the eighteenth dynasty, Egyptians drew animals to represent laughable qualities in people; caricature could be found in Hindu drawings, on the walls of Pompeii or on Greek vases; medieval missals and gargoyles spouting rainwater from the cathedrals continued the comic tradition. Visual mockery has a long tradition behind it. It often existed on the margins of art; at first only the outcasts of society, slaves, sinners, parasites and other humble folk were its targets; and usually as types, rather than as individuals. Pieter Breughel the Elder (1525–1569) continued this tradition: his scenes from peasant life ridiculed his subjects, though with little malice. Doctors and lawyers and other members of the lucrative professions were caricatured towards the close of the Middle Ages; the *Dance of Death,* with its portrayal of various sinners, anticipated modern satire. During the Reformation satire began to be used as an instrument of propaganda: at Luther's request the Pope was ruthlessly abused in Cranach's woodcuts. Here we find the origins of modern 'illustrated libel'[1] — crude assaults on the opponent which score propaganda points.

When caricature started being used for religious or political propaganda early in the sixteenth century, it moved away from the gentle mockery of, say, Breughel, and character assassination of their subjects became the aim of the artists. In the same century, however, modern portrait caricature, which could be malicious without being abusive, was established as an art form: it distorted by exaggerating the most characteristic features of its subject. Annibale Carracci (1560–1609), better known as a master of the conventional style, invented the caricature, and became its leading practitioner. Carracci is reported to have said:

Is not the caricaturist's task exactly the same as the classical artist's? Both see the lasting truth beneath the

Peace, An Idyll, Honoré Daumier, *Le Charivari*, 1871 (left) and *The Last Dance*, French, 1944 (right)
The medieval theme of the dance of death: the stark, sombre way Honoré Daumier used it in his drawing contrasts with the more explicit, ephemeral cartoon published soon after the liberation of Paris in 1944, showing Pierre Laval, the French premier and collaborator, and Marshal Pétain, the nominal head of state, accompanying Hitler's dance on the accordion.

surface of mere outward appearance. Both try to help nature accomplish its plan. The one may strive to visualize the perfect form and to realize it in his work, the other to grasp the perfect deformity, and thus reveal the very essence of a personality. A good caricature, like every work of art, is more true to life than reality itself.[2]

The Renaissance had opened up the world of experimentation in art. Leonardo da Vinci (1452–1519) drew grotesque, ugly heads; at the court of Rudolf II in Prague, Arcimboldo painted striking portraits composed entirely of fruit and vegetables. Neither artist had the intention of making a satiric point but such experiments helped other artists to discover that faithful representation of likeness could be misleading, and that the true caricaturist aims at the essential characteristics of his subject, making him ridiculous by concentrating on them. Features as well as expression on a face are his targets, and stark economy of line his technique. There is a balance between humour and malice in caricature; it shows the viewer how to take a fresh look at a face. Aping, clowning and mimicry are its equivalent; a subsidiary pleasure from jokes, Freud tells us, is that they may produce new pleasures by sublimating aggression and suppressed emotions. When caricaturists are given the licence to attack persons who are powerful in a society, they cut them down to size and in so doing they humanize them. The distance between the viewer and the

object of caricature is diminished and tension between them is removed.

When caricature reached England in the eighteenth century, William Hogarth (1697–1764) described it as a more or less sophisticated joke. Hogarth himself said that his work had nothing to do with caricature, because he was not striving for witty comparisons of unlike things but wanted to reveal character. But Hogarth and his art — the *Rake's Progress* series and *The Four Stages of Cruelty* are probably the best-known examples — gave caricature a new life. James Gillray (1757–1815), by reducing politicians to simple formulae, became probably the first cartoonist in the modern sense; he was a master of invective, whose subjects — Pitt, Fox, Sheridan or Napoleon — are still as alive as they were in his day. Both Hogarth and Gillray were working in a similar tradition as Pieter Breughel in his copperplate etchings of 1563, the *Dinner of the Poor* and the *Dinner of the Rich*. They brought social and political conflict into focus, and established the ground-rules for moral-didactic satire.

In nineteenth-century France caricature used a range of techniques similar to those it had used in eighteenth-century England; but now, for the first time, it was used in mass-circulation journals. Because of the immediacy of print, caricature could be more topical and reach a far wider audience than it had ever done before. In

Defender of Paris, Abel Pann, September 1914 (left) and *A Frog He Would A-Wooing Go*, Philip Zec, *Daily Mirror*, 30 October 1941 (right)
Writers of fables as well as cartoonists use animals to represent human characteristics: the hedgehog — General Gallieni — defended Paris in 1914, during the first battle of the Marne. Another Frenchman, Pierre Laval, was depicted as a toad by Philip Zec at a time when Laval, down on his political luck, tried to draw even closer to Hitler's Germany.

1830 Charles Phillipon started a comic weekly, *La Caricature* and then a daily, *Le Charivari*. They were the ancestors of satirical magazines over all the world, and employed the leading artists in Paris. Honoré Daumier introduced social satire of a distinctly modern character: he created several types — Robert Macaire, for instance, a corrupt speculator of diabolical dimensions — who mockingly questioned the social structure of contemporary society. Daumier and Doré, Grandville and Gavarni, most of the masters of caricature, worked for Phillipon's magazines.

By the time *Punch* was established in London in 1842, there had taken place in England a swing away from the 'coarseness' of the eighteenth century. Caricature 'put on kid gloves, and sprayed its chest with lavender'.[3] Cartoons by, say, John Lush and John Tenniel became both circumspect and respectful — the development of the law of libel may have helped the artists to be more cautious. Caricature became 'cartooning' and satirical comment was transformed into humorous reporting. When David Low, a New Zealander who had worked in Australia, came to London in 1919, his directness shocked his public, still accustomed to cartooning rather than hard-hitting political satire.

Low commented on English caricature as he found it in the 1920s:

Australian wit and humour, though following English forms, had had, besides our native tartness, a touch of American smartness. The English, by all the evidence, had much more appreciation of humour than of wit. Wit was rather the diversion of the intellectuals, narrowed to more or less obscure or esoteric references and associations. In 1920 there was no radio and Hollywood was young; and the British masses still had not only music, songs, plays, pictures but especially their own local jokes, farce and broad comedy, none of it as yet overlaid by streamlined American imports. The traditions were plainly discernible in the survival of the popular old robust jokes about drunks, buttocks and mothers-in-law, etc., even when their aptness had departed, and in the love of puns and wordplay, and endless repetition, and comic 'characters'. It was true that in respect of the art of caricature there had been much evolution and departure from tradition. By the time the world arrived at 1920 the original ribald rowdy fun of the old masters in this department, Gillray and Rowlandson, had been considerably watered down. Lush, Doyle, Tenniel, Sambourne and Partridge had rubbed the rough places off the genuine article and substituted dignity and grace for strength and power in political caricature; so that one no longer laughed — if one laughed — from the stomach, but from the front teeth. The translation of the of caricature from the periodical to the daily newspaper had begun in many ways an even more restricting and emasculating change. Satire was shooed up a back street as too vulgar for the vulgus, and its place was filled by facetiousness and whimsy.

In Germany, when Hitler and his followers first

emerged in the beerhalls and the streets of Munich in the early 1920s, the art of caricature was well-established. Its development was perhaps slower than it had been in France or England because the obstacles in its path were greater. Dialect created a barrier; the widely divergent local dialects made communication between Germans difficult, even when they came together in one state after 1870. Indeed, such local humour as existed in the various parts of Germany not only took place behind the barriers of a dialect, but the dialect was its vehicle: it was local, and it did not travel well.

Nor did the Germans have a significant literary tradition with a rich comic seam. *Simplicius Simplicissimus,* written in the seventeenth century during the Thirty Years War, had accidental humour scattered in its pages. Goethe could sometimes be witty, but it would be difficult to describe him as a funny writer. Heinrich Heine's satire was shot through by too much solemnity; in the twentieth century, only Thomas Mann's *Felix Krull* may be ranked as a major humorous novel.[4]

The Germans had no Villon, Cervantes, Twain or Hašek; their playwrights could not match Shakespeare's sense of fun. Friedrich Schiller, in an essay entitled *The Theatre As a Moral Institution* (1784), advocated stark seriousness in theatre, unrelieved by comedy. The work of Wilhelm Busch and Hans-Christian Morgenstern,

the latter a witty poet with a talent for clever punning, the former a cartoonist and poet with a keen eye for human foibles, was relegated to the status of a minor art. In a way, greatness, seriousness and the tragic sense were either identified as being synonymous or at least lived in a close and uncomfortable proximity.

It is not surprising that the Germans acquired a reputation abroad for lacking a sense of humour. Their philosophers, from Herder on, made much of national characteristics without allowing for a broad diversity of character in each nation; and humourlessness was one of the labels which has stuck to the Germans. It was deserved. Prussia and its Hohenzollern dynasty had, during the nineteenth century, developed an image of stern pomposity, but even here there was the enclave of the Berliners who developed their own urban sense of the ridiculous; yet again, it was closely linked with the Berlin dialect and therefore difficult for the outsider. Lack of humour may have been a Prussian quality but it was not one shared by, say, the Rhinelanders or the Bavarians. It was Hitler's misfortune that he and his movement originated in Munich, the capital of Bavaria, but the art of caricature benefited from that chance connection.

Hitler, his party and his state, gave rise to a rich harvest of political cartoons and satire. The time, the place, as well as the target were right. Hitler and the Nazis provided the artists with a broad and

From *L'Heure*, 1937 (far left)
and *1938's Four Horsemen*,
Vaughn Shoemaker, *Chicago
Daily News*, 1938 (left)
*The personified globe,
handcuffed and carrying an
olive branch, waits for Hitler's
axe to fall as his warlike aims
become more apparent. The
French cartoon of 1937 deals
with the same theme as the
American drawing of the next
year entitled the* Four
Horsemen, *who handle the
globe as a ball in their
aggressive football charge.*

The Beast is Unleashed, Jean
Veber, 1914 (right)
*The beast of 1914 showed as
much aggressive energy as the
four horsemen of 1938 were to.
The earlier cartoon is more
effective, probably because the
beast's target is only implied.*

La Brute est lachée

clearly visible target. The attack was launched at first in Germany, and more specifically in Munich, in the early 1920s. After 1933, Hitler's regime was to be taken seriously; his government was neither self-confident nor tolerant enough to allow itself to be ridiculed by people who lived in the area under its control. The centre of the attack moved abroad, and, indeed, by 1933 enough was known about Hitler and his regime to make attacks on it from abroad effective and intelligible.

The Weimar republic also favoured the satirist and the political cartoonist. In the Great War, Prussian military virtues — unbending, serious and mean — had not delivered their early promise to the Germans. An alternative for the unifying principle used by Bismarck, the military strength of Prussia, had to be found. The Weimar Republic experimented with republican democracy and with socialism: a period of experiment which was terminated by Hitler. In a way, the gaiety and frivolity of the Weimar period, and its artistic achievements, mocked the serious face of war and of defeat. The war and its aftermath also exacerbated the political and social tensions which had accumulated in the pre-war period.

In a way similar to William Hogarth's eighteenth-century England, or Daumier's nineteenth-century France, Wilhelmine and then post-World War I Germany provided a rich territory for social satire. Industrial revolution after the

unification of Germany in 1870 was perhaps more abrupt, faster and more intensive than anywhere else in Europe. Socially, religiously and politically diverse parts of the nation confronted each other in one state. In the quarter of a century before the war Germany's gross national product more than doubled, production of steel shot ahead that of Britain, and the proportion of Germans disposing of a taxable income increased from 30 to 60 per cent. Germany became a country of stark contrasts, where the structures of political and social realities were not yet reconciled and were overlaid by the camouflage of tradition, habit and acceptance. The war created new, vast forms of industrial and military organizations, which diminished the value of the individual. Modernity existed side-by-side with anachronism, feudal elements with progressive social measures, and industrial achievement with rural backwardness. Writing of the pre-World War I period, a German historian remarked: 'There were anachronistic features in the total picture of imperial Germany, but these came from a quarter other than the economic or social reality. Over this hard-working country, seemingly so sure of its future, with rapidly growing metropolises and industrial areas, there arched a peculiarly romantic sky whose darkness was populated by mythical figures and ancient deities. Germany's backwardness was chiefly ideological in its nature.'[5]

Communists Fall and Shares Rise, George Grosz, from *Gott mit uns, 1919* (left), *Cross Section,* George Grosz, from *Ecce Homo,* 1920 (centre), and *He's Called Hermann,* Bert (right)

The brutality and confusion of Germany after World War I were strikingly reflected in George Grosz's drawings. Note the little uniformed figure wearing a helmet with a swastika, waiting on the sidelines, on the right-hand margin of Cross Section. Communists Fall and Shares Rise *refers to Bloody Week (10–17 January 1919) when regular and irregular troops of the Republic crushed the communist 'Spartacists', who had occupied the imperial palace in Berlin. Bert's caricature of Göring mocks his involvement with a workers' party in spite of his patrician connections. His 'decoration' is labelled 'Hitler Paintbrush I. Class'.*

To the brashness of the new Germany, with Berlin in search of a role as a world capital, to Protestant Prussia and the north, Catholic Bavaria in a way provided a counterpoint. While royal Munich comfortably assumed the status of a provincial town, it retained certain advantages. Its comparative, easy-going freedom, which accommodated eccentricity and social idiosyncrasy, and its large artistic colony, which benefited from liberal laws concerning residence for foreigners, stood in stark contrast to the straight-laced ways of Prussia. *Simplicissimus,* the leading satirical magazine, could only be born and prosper in Munich; it drew on the considerable talent concentrated in the local artistic colony. Appropriately, on 1 April 1896 Albert Langen, the publisher, and the artist, Thomas Theodor Heine, asked potential contributors to dinner at Matheserbräu, a comfortable Munich restaurant. *Simplicissimus*, a cheap (10 pfennig) weekly magazine in colour, soon appeared and very quickly established a reputation for high-class mockery of the pompous and contradictory society. The earliest and best cartoons concerning Hitler and his movement appeared in *Simplicissimus.*

Soon after the end of World War I Hitler and the National Socialists became known in Munich, but it was not their intention merely to take their place among the gallery of Bavarian eccentrics. They were serious, and wanted to be taken seriously, but many artists in Munich found it difficult to do so. Indeed, some of the earliest clashes between Hitler and his opponents concerned art and aesthetics, rather than politics. Hitler made no secret of his views on art, which were of a positive, philistine kind; and German artists, we shall see, often ridiculed them.

The artists who attacked Hitler, inside and outside Germany from 1923 to 1945, were favoured by their time bacause of the medium they worked in. They appeared in both mass circulation daily newspapers (abroad after the mid-1930s) and in the more specialized, or low-circulation magazines and pamphlets (mostly in Germany up until 1933). There was a broad distinction within this medium. On the whole, cartoonists who worked for the mass-circulation daily press were under pressure to deal with problems thrown up by the fast-moving flow of the daily news. Their reactions were, therefore, sometimes ephemeral. There was also in the years just preceding and during the war a lot of borrowing of ideas and themes, including borrowing across national frontiers. Nevertheless, there were notable talented artists working for the dailies: David Low in England and David Fitzpatrick in America dealt not only with the daily news and its background, but they used them to expose the basic nature of their own and of international society.

Other graphic artists of distinction, whose work sometimes appeared in low-circulation magazines or pamphlets, had joined in the attack on Hitler and his creations somewhat earlier. Painters George Grosz and Josef Čapek were among them; graphic artists such as Paul Weber or Theodor Heine; and an innovative artist whose work eluded categorization: John Heartfield. They took a longer-term view of their target. By dissecting and diminishing the Nazi movement, their work often transcended its central European setting. Although depicting specific events, their caricatures also commented on general issues of life and death, peace and war, sense and lunacy.

Nevertheless, it could have been expected that the caricatures might now be so dated as to be either incomprehensible, or at least difficult to decipher. The high turnover of twentieth-century news might have created a stream in which even the strongest artist would have drowned. This did not happen, because in terms of sheer graphical mastery and inventiveness, some of the work was of high and enduring quality. As a running commentary on Hitler, his movement and his state, the work of the great caricaturists was thoughtful, often highly perceptive and influential. Caricature helped to shape attitudes to Hitler and his creations inside and outside Germany; and perhaps it had a long-term effect on the historiography of the period.

Increasing the Nordic Race, Frantisek Bidlo, 1937 (above);
Faithful Nibelungs, Bert, 1936 (centre) and *Single-Dish Meal,*
Bert, 1934 (right)
*The exhibition of anti-fascist cartoons in Prague in April–May
1934 exposed the criminal nature of Hitler's regime, as well as
capturing the true character of Nazi leaders. But until this time,
that knowledge appears to have been confined to central
Europe: the rest of the world, including western Europe, was
still largely ignorant of the Nazi threat.* Faithful Nibelungs *shows
the kind of funeral for Ernst Röhm that would have been
designed by a Nazi admirer of Wagner, while his* 'Das
Einkopfgericht' *('one-headed dish') makes a pun on*
Eintopfgericht, *a single-dish meal popular at Nazi fund-raising
functions.*

It is easier to assess the cartoons for their
accuracy as reflections of the Nazi phenomenon
than for their impact on their audience. But there is
no doubt that they helped, by their cumulative
effect, to mount a broadly based campaign, both in
Europe and especially in America, against Hitler's
creations. In Germany the campaign failed when
Nazi censorship was imposed in 1933. Yet even
before this the caricatures sometimes failed when
the simplification process essential to caricature
produced a misleading impression and the thrust
of the point missed the target. Early on when Hitler
was perceived, for instance, as a windbag, as a
man who added up to no more than the noises he
made, the assessment of him was wrong. Most of
the time, however, the image of Hitler presented in
caricature was chillingly accurate.

In May 1934 the first exhibition of anti-Nazi
cartoons was mounted in Prague. It included the
work of German artists, many of whom had, in
1933, been silenced, exiled or imprisoned, and a
number of Czech cartoonists. More than a year
after Hitler's accession to power, it showed a
comprehensive, and basically accurate, picture of
the Nazi phenomenon. It stressed the inherent
inhumanity and cruelty of Hitler's movement; it was
detailed and reliable on the racial policies of the
movement and of the new Nazi state; it was
perceptive of the main characteristics of its
leaders — picking on Hitler's faithlessness

towards his former associates, or Göring's vanity,
or the pretentiousness of Goebbels' thinking. But
the main thrust of the exhibition was to promote a
strong warning on the basic criminality of Hitler's
regime. At that time the warning had only a limited
effect. Some of the reasons for this are suggested
on the pages dealing with the emigration from
Germany to Prague of the artists who opposed the
Nazi state.

It so happened that the best anti-Nazi cartoons
were also the most lasting. Nevertheless, in the
early stages of Hitler's movement only a few artists
concerned themselves with it. As the movement
grew from its Bavarian origins, mockery of it also
broadened, but before 1933 this was largely
confined to a few quality newspapers and
periodicals in Germany and Central Europe,
comment in the popular press being negligible; the
best examples of this Central European view were
on show at the 1934 Prague exhibition. It was
largely the work of left-wing or left-of-centre
artists, the natural enemies of Hitler. Only after
Hitler came to power on 30 January 1933 and after
his first foreign policy moves did the visual
campaign against him become truly international.
But as the geographical base of the campaign
broadened it began losing some of its earlier sharp
focus and some of its subtlety and the picture of
Hitler and the Nazis was frequently blurred or
stereotyped. There were, of course, exceptions:

Low in Britain, Fitzpatrick in America, Efimov in Russia and Hoffmeister in exile. For the later period between 1935 and 1945, we try to give the best examples of cartoons which formed a part of a continuous stream of ephemera; again the best of them seem to have survived the intervening decades comparatively unharmed; they give a light-hearted view of a period of European history when light-heartedness was not a common quality of life.

The Nazi period coincided with the primacy of the press among the mass media and with the beginning of its decline. In the 1930s sound broadcasting began to challenge the privileged position of the press, but it came into its own only in the concluding stages of the war. Television was in its infancy; not until after the war did it diminish the value of older, visual aids to understanding the world. Since the end of World War II, the art of the political cartoon — and of political satire — has declined in Europe and in America, along with the influence of the press. Occasional flashes of incisive wit still occur in cartoons: but a sustained, high-quality campaign against mindlessness and inhumanity, such as was conducted against Hitler, his movement, and then his state, is now more difficult to mount. The absence of a suitable target is only a part of the explanation.

Newspapers are are no longer the leading source of the latest news, and political cartoons are not not at their best when they deal only with background material. Cartoonists now often concentrate on parochial or personal issues; subjects with wider, international implications are either ignored or domesticated. Television has drawn some of the talent and much of the attention of the audience. And because television is a selectively descriptive rather than an analytical medium, and the product of a team rather than of individual talent, it has not developed a form which would bring the news together with incisive, artistic statements concerning the main political and moral trends behind the news: the kind of statements which political cartoonists and satirists often made about Nazi Germany with supreme skill.

John Bull's War Aim, Bernard Partridge, *Punch,* 18 October 1939

Young Hitler: The Making of a Famous Monster

In his youth Hitler saw himself as being cut out for some high mission. He daydreamed, wasted a lot of time and despised formal education and the dull pursuits of ordinary people. His view of himself and his way of life conformed to the romantic, Central European concept of the artist as a young man. There were only two ways out of that predicament: fame or death.

Perhaps Hitler's early failure as an artist provides the clue to his need for self-assertion. In October 1907, when he was eighteen and with little formal education (due more to lack of self-discipline rather than opportunity), Hitler applied for the drawing examination at the Academy in Vienna. It was noted, on the classification list, that 'The following gentlemen were not admitted to the examination . . . Adolf Hitler, Braunau b. 20 April 1889, German, Catholic, Father civil servant, upper rank, four grades of *Realschule.* Few heads submitted. Sample drawing unsatisfactory.'[1]

It was a severe shock to Hitler who was disappointed for the first time in the pursuit of his ambition; nor was it to be the last time. Although he made no attempt to acquire any practical training, Adolf Hitler tried once again in September 1908 to enter the Academy. This time he was not even admitted to the preliminary test. Hitler, who had neglected formal education when it was on offer to him, failed to secure a place for himself in a

system which he despised from then on. Thus was born his lifelong resentment against academic education in the creative arts; he maintained that true genius (such as his) could not be accommodated by the system.

But his tastes in art curiously trapped the young Hitler. In his view, academic 'pipsqueaks' could not tolerate genius; but strangely enough, although Hitler's ambition lay in the visual arts, he had little appreciation of them. His passion was music. He immersed himself in the music of Richard Wagner and sometimes went to the opera night after night. The Master of Bayreuth provided Hitler with consolation, feeding his vague, boundless ambition. The romantic adaptation of German myths, their unthinking, blind heroism, their hints of incestuous love, their passion leading unfailingly to disaster and death, provided the young Hitler with an alternative to the narrow, bourgeois mentality with which he had grown up — and a reason for rejecting it. Wagner and his music were to remain his lifelong passion.

The important experiments in music which were being made in Vienna before 1914 were ignored by Hitler, or else were unknown to him. The work of Schönberg and his pupils, Alban Berg and Anton von Webern, of Gustav Mahler and of Richard Strauss, passed Hitler by. Innovations in the visual arts equally made no impact on him. Oskar Kokoschka, Gustav Klimt and Egon Schiele had as

disturbing an effect on the artistic world of Vienna as did the musicians. Hitler, however, admired the conventional, academic painting of artists such as Rudolf von Alt, Anselm Feuerbach and Karl Mottmann. In architecture, a profession towards which Hitler had some ill-defined ambitions, his tastes were also of the most conventional, conservative kind. In 1911, Adolf Loos, the architect who was young Kokoschka's patron, completed his absolutely modern, flat façade in the Michaelerplatz, directly facing the highly ornamental Hofburg of the Habsburgs. Hitler had no interest in such experiments, preferring the conventional urban designs of his time.

A few sketches, posters and small watercolours by Hitler from the time he spent in Vienna still survive, bearing witness to his tastes and talent. They were sold by the more enterprising of the inmates of the Vienna hostels for men where Hitler lived to anyone who cared to buy them. They have the careful, unimaginative quality of picture postcards — from which, indeed, many of them were copied. When Hitler moved from Vienna to Munich shortly before the outbreak of World War I, he carried on with his undistinguished trade. In a pedantic, cautious way, he concentrated on physical detail; every blade of grass, every brick, every cloud in the sky were recorded to the best of his ability. Wassily Kandinsky, Paul Klee and Franz Marc lived in Schwabing, the same quarter of

Munich as Hitler, as did several contributors to the satirical magazine *Simplicissimus.* (Incidentally Lenin, whose regime later became Hitler's main adversary, had lived in the same street — Schleissheimer Strasse — where Hitler became a tenant of a tailor called Popp in 1913.) But the artistic and intellectual excitement of Munich failed to interest Hitler. By now, he may have been aware of his deficiencies as an artist. He was unable to reveal his visions and anxieties in his art because he had neither the symbols nor the technique to make such expression possible. Most of the German artists who later ridiculed Hitler — George Grosz, Paul Weber, Karl Arnold and John Heartfield, for instance — had the advantage of a formal artistic education and the ability to express themselves through the artistic medium. Hitler's later denunciation of them was coloured by envy and resentment, for they had succeeded where he failed.

Hitler found his first personal redemption in the Great War. At the end of it he was blinded by gas, but had two Iron Crosses to his credit, one awarded to him in the first and the other in the last year of the war. After the war Hitler saw himself, among other things, as the proper heir to Prussia and its military virtues. Most of his artistic adversaries — and their first skirmishes took place some five years after the end of the war — had also done military service. But they did not see the

war as a means of personal fulfilment, nor did they accept Germany's defeat in a state of blind fury. For them, the war was a gigantic blunder organized and licensed by the state. They — and many others — could not take seriously Hitler's and his followers' hysterical tirades when they were first delivered in the streets and the beer cellars of Munich in the early 1920s. Although the Great War was an experience Hitler had in common with the artists who later ridiculed him it was his attitude to defeat in war which divided him from them. At the end of the war 'in the chaos of collapse, Germany assumed the shape of an enormously magnified men's hostel'.[2] It was at this time that Hitler decided to become a politician.

Hitler had a mixed bag of phobias. They included cities and their industries, American technology, the birthrate of the Slavs, big corporations, revolutionary Bolshevism; they were all, in Hitler's words, 'signs of decay of a slowly ebbing world'. His hatred of the Jews linked his anxieties and made them coherent. As he was a brilliant speaker he could address himself to similar anxieties in his audience. His energy, his flair for organization and his ability to manipulate crises helped him to build up a small but solid power base in Munich. In his first letter, on 17 September 1921, soon after the party conferred dictatorial powers on him, as the chairman of the NSDAP — *die Nationalsozialistische Deutsche Arbeiterpartei* (National Socialist German Workers' Party) — he concerned himself largely with the central symbol of his small party: the swastika party badge, which members were to wear at all times.

In the provincial circumstances of Munich Hitler remained socially inept. It may be that he tried to profit from his awkwardness. A few of the more adventurous Munich hostesses invited him to their houses: after his early political successes, they wanted to take a closer look at the somewhat repellent but curious young man. He usually arrived late, brought too many flowers, talked too much, too abruptly, or not at all. His watery eyes stared at the world from above a nose underscored by an unusually narrow moustache. One observer noted that when he talked to General Ludendorff he rose at the end of each sentence the war hero uttered, bowing slightly and saying: 'Very well, Your Excellency.' In his early Munich days, he was seen wearing an old tail coat, brown shoes and a rucksack on his back. Even when he was better dressed, his appearance was no less striking. He favoured a velour hat, riding boots and breeches, a trench coat; a riding whip and a cartridge belt and revolver completed his costume. The SA — the *Sturmabteilung* — Hitler's private army, was founded soon after he had taken full control of the party in the summer of 1921; its members imitated Hitler. Their loyalty was to their leader, rather than to a political programme.

Adolf and August — the Munich Circus,
anon., *Simplicissimus,* 1927 (right) and
Mythical Hero, Stephen Roth (above)
*At one point Simplicissimus saw Hitler as
a political lightweight, a circus performer
appealing to exactly the same Munich
audience as the traditional Bavarian
clown, August. Roth presents him as an
ambiguous Hamlet-figure, holding in place
of Yorick's skull a symbolic composite of
the hoped-for sources of Nazi strength
— the army, the Ruhr industrialists and
the admirers of* Mein Kampf.

In the Hofbräukeller, Paul Weber, from *Hitler — A German Fate,* 1932 (left) and *All Blown Up and Nowhere to Go,* David Low, 1933 (below) *Two ways of looking at Hitler as a bubble: one sinister, the other comic.*

Hitler   **ALL BLOWN UP AND NOWHERE TO GO**

Those historians who argued later that Hitler and
his state were something extraordinary,
transcending human categories, almost renounced
their right to analyse it: or, at least, they found it
easier to describe the phenomenon than to explain
it. Hitler's evil and devilish — inhuman — nature
was the clue to his character and the nature of his
regime.

George Grosz's Hitler, drawn in the year of
Hitler's failed *putsch* in Bavaria in 1923, told a
different story. Grosz's Hitler is a more human
figure but divided against himself. The *Urmensch*
from the dank, dark forest — his name, of course,
was Siegfried Hitler — who had a necklace of teeth
around his neck and wore a furry shift, would not
have plastered his hair down so carefully, and cut
his moustache in such an odd way. There was a
smug and belligerent expression on Hitler's face,
an expression which should not have been on the
face of one of the heroes of the great German
myth. It properly belonged to the face of, say, a
member of the *Turnverein* — the nationalist
society of German gymnasts — or perhaps an
army NCO would have worn it in his more relaxed
moments. There was a dangerous, downward
curve about Hitler's mouth. Grosz was pointing out
Hitler's ludicrous mysticism and its underlying
banality, in a way only possible for someone who
was familiar with the phenomenon, having
observed it closely in its own setting. Grosz's

dislike for the object of Hitler's admiration — the
German army — is neatly expressed in another
caricature. In the drawing of the barrack-square
exercise the automatic, uniform quality of the
troops is contrasted with the ugliness and brutality
of the officers and NCOs.

Soulless military, tyrannical schoolmasters,
greedy businessmen marked by self-importance,
alcohol, or poisoned eroticism, were the target of
Grosz's satire. There was hate in his work, but he
was not a malicious cartoonist; his satire was pure
and direct. His 1920s collections *The Face of the
Ruling Class (Das Gesicht der herrschenden
Klasse),* as well as *Ecce Homo,* show Grosz's art
at its most powerful and distinctive.

He would have been unable to live in a country
run by a movement which embodied everything he
abhorred. World War I was a generalized idiocy for
Grosz and a personal salvation for Hitler; Prussian
military virtues, grafted onto lower-middle class
values of pettiness and meanness, had been
Grosz's target for some time before Hitler came to
power.

Grosz was able to translate his desires,
anxieties and preferences into the terms of the
visual arts. Hitler, however much he may have
wished to do so, was unable to perform that feat.
But he became supremely skilled at expressing
himself in terms of politics. He came to embody —
more than Mussolini, the fascist leader who had

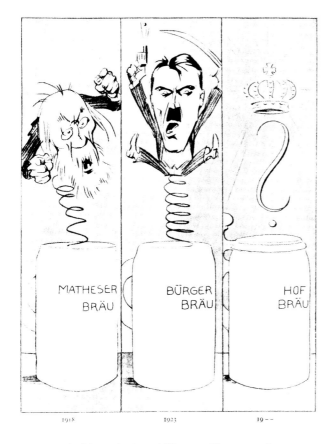

succeeded long before Hitler, or Franco, who came to power partly with Hitler's assistance — the fascist type of politician. The war had educated and freed Hitler; the post-war years made him into a politician. Though he had 'come from nothing' to lead a great nation, Hitler started on his political career in Munich with certain advantages.

GEORGE GROSZ, the son of a Berlin publican, was born in 1893. His parents were Prussian Lutherans who moved in 1898 from Berlin to Stolp in Pomerania, where the father kept house and bar for the local free-masons. Grosz's childhood was spent in the limiting meanness of a Prussian provincial town and sometimes his work looked like an analysis of that narrowness, at other times a revenge on it. When he was eleven he started going on sketching trips in the countryside; soon after this he acquired an admiration for *Kitsch,* the trashy, cheap romantic artefacts by the 'soap painters'. He collected such objects all his life. He spent two years at the Dresden Academy studying art, and developed there an admiration for the modern movement, especially Nolde and Van Gogh, against the advice of his teachers. He also became acquainted with the work of the *Brücke* school in Dresden, and the *Blaue Reiter* group in Munich. When he was seventeen the satirical weekly supplement of *Berliner Tageblatt* accepted a drawing by him. Early in his career Grosz tried his hand at designing typefaces, wallpaper, book jackets and restaurant menus. His first serious drawings and poems were published in 1915 in *Die Neue Jugend* edited by Wieland Herzfelde, John Heartfield's brother, and in the anti-war magazine, *Die Aktion.* Grosz came to regard the war as an orgy of immorality, and it contributed to the development of his rather misanthropic personality and his sceptical, individualist attitudes.

In 1916 he began depicting the evil and corruption of German society and the social misfits that the war had produced: war cripples, war widows, and drunks. After the war, Grosz took part in the Dada movement, the forerunner of surrealism. In 1933 he went to teach at the Arts Students League, a leading art school in New York, and spent most of the rest of his life in the USA. He returned to Berlin in May 1959 and died there two months later.

If Soldiers Were Not Such 'Dummköpfe' They Would Have Run Away From Me Long Ago, 1923 (above); *White General, Die Pleite*, November 1923 (above right); *For the Fatherland — To the Slaughterhouse, Der Knuppel*, 25 July 1934 (below right) and *Pillars of Society*, 1926 (far right); all by George Grosz
Grosz's best works delineated the corruption and decadence of Weimar Germany and his hatred of war and militarism. His caricatures reveal the features of the new ruling class, grafted on to the old one and ready to espouse the Nazi cause. By 1934 the 'new' Germany was well established with life and work regimented to a degree never before experienced in the country. While arms manufacturers grew rich, for those who stepped out of line there were the concentration camps.

Hitler Cancels the Treaty of Versailles, Swiss, *Nebelspalter*, 1935?

The Nazi Movement

Hitler had an intuitive understanding of the many German anxieties. Most recently, there was the shock of defeat, and of the 'syphilitic peace', in the inelegant phrase of the Nazi daily, *Völkischer Beobachter* (the Versailles Peace Treaty combined moral disapproval with the demand for reparations in the same paragraph). The fear of revolution, which had haunted the middle classes in central Europe since the revolution in France, was given a new impetus by the events in Russia. Reports of horrifying atrocities started reaching Germany when the Soviet state was established in 1917. Hitler thought of Russia as the 'brutal power colossus', and many middle-class Germans feared that, equipped with the Marxist doctrine, Russia was in a better position than ever to issue a comprehensive challenge to Germany's traditional values.

Twentieth-century modernity had, for many Germans, an ugly, repulsive face. Hostility to both industry and to its most welcoming host, the large city, the megalopolis, increased. Large corporations and department stores were pushing the small businessmen out: together with academics and other formerly prosperous members of the middle class, they and the white collar workers (the 'non-commissioned officers of capitalism') felt under threat. Modernity was vast and foreign, un-German: it could only lead to a standardized, ant-like existence. Its strange anonymity was expressed, for the opponents of modernity, in the technical matter-of-factness of the Bauhaus or in the style of Adolf Loos or Le Corbusier, in pre-fabricated building, in modern art, in tubular steel furniture. The term *Kulturbolschewismus* (Cultural Bolshevism), a description used for the modern movements in the arts, was later replaced by the Nazi concept of *entartete Kunst* (decadent art). The bourgeoisie was also frightened by Eugen Friedländer's *Sexual Ethics of Communism,* which declared marriage to be an evil spawn of capitalism, which would be done away with together with unreasonable prohibitions against homosexuality, incest or abortion.

The Soviet Union, or rather *Bolschewismus* and, more remotely, *Amerikanismus* were somehow connected, in the minds of the German middle classes, with threatening modernity and the parallel decline of German values, especially those affecting the family and the state. The Jews also were seen as being linked with the causes of modernity and of revolution: their achievements were based on flexibility, mobility and the towns; they were therefore unlikely to be either loyal to or closely linked with the soil. Nevertheless, the threat to German values, it was thought, came mainly from the outside, either from the east or from the west. The east, of course, looked more threatening because of the revolutionary regime in

Russia. Although Oswald Spengler, the prophet of doom for the west, called on the Germans to fight against 'the England within us', Russia, the 'fourth dimension', presented middle-class Germans with their most challenging threat. The various postwar vigilante groups and the *Freikorps* (armed bands principally composed of ex-servicemen excluded from the regular army) prepared themselves to fight communist revolution.

In addition, Hitler, as a young man in Vienna, had experience of German political isolation. For decades before the outbreak of World War I, the Slavs in the Austrian part of the Austro-Hungarian monarchy, and especially the Czechs, had made political and economic advances, sometimes at the expense of the Germans; by the time Hitler arrived in Vienna, there was considerable lobbying by German political parties and leaders in the Habsburg Empire who opposed the Slav pretensions or who wanted to take the Germans out of the Empire and attach them to the newly united *Reich.* Hitler himself avoided military service in 1913 in the Austrian army and then a year later, served in the German one.

Hitler knew his audience well, and he learned how to put his views across to it. The passages on propaganda in *Mein Kampf* reach a level of clarity and simplicity unequalled in other parts of the book. Propaganda had to reach the largest amount of people, and therefore had to appeal and be intelligible to the lowest common denominator. It could contain lies: if lies were repeated often enough, they became acceptable and acquired the ring of truth. Hitler found it unnecessary to draw any distinction, as the Marxist communist parties usually did, between propaganda and agitation. For them, propaganda was the vehicle for the transmission of Marxist doctrine, whereas agitation was a minor art in comparison, creating the day-to-day political mood. Hitler had no comprehensive political doctrine to offer; he translated the mood of the time into political action. And he soon came to understand the link between violence and publicity: the early clashes of his followers with their opponents in Munich provided the newspapers with good copy, and the Nazis with publicity for their cause. Hitler used the connections between propaganda and violence consistently, with icy deliberation. The cartoon by Ente (p. 31), where two Nazis shout simple slogans—'Heil Hitler' and 'Down with Jewry'—at Hitler's rough, mechanical bidding, illustrates the nature and quality of Nazi propaganda.

The art of Paul Weber, one of the foremost German graphic artists and illustrators, threw a sharp light on the nature of the Nazi movement when Hitler was on the way to power. The visionary, prophetic quality of his work stands out in the campaign against Hitler and National Socialism.

THE SOURCE.

For Weber as for other German artists, including another leading cartoonist, Karl Arnold, World War I was a formative experience. In Weber's case the gloomy, nightmarish quality never lifted from his work, which remained dominated by the twin themes of death and material destruction.

Weber began a close collaboration with Ernst Niekisch, a radical publisher, and briefly the Premier of Bavaria, in 1928. In 1932 he illustrated Niekisch's anti-Nazi pamphlet, entitled *Hitler — Ein deutsches Verhängnis* (Hitler — a German Fate). It sold 50,000 copies before Hitler came to power in January 1933, and contained some of the best work by Weber on the National Socialist movement. It is visionary, prophetic, and haunted by a feeling of doom. The frontispiece boldly depicts death in the uniform of an *SA-Mann*. The Hitler greeting, the wide-open mouth, left hand on the buckle of the belt: a characteristic, ugly pose. The death figure towers over the fanaticized masses and the SA standards; the background is gloomy, menacing, with ravens circling over some unimaginable disaster. The central illustration in Niekisch's anti-Nazi pamphlet is simply entitled *The Fate*. It complements and explains the first picture. It depicts an enormous coffin with a swastika which is where *SA-Mann* is bidding the masses to go (p. 32).

Despite the strikingly direct visible symbols of the Nazi movement, its ultimate aims were ambiguous. There was a lack of definition about Hitler and his National Socialist movement from the beginning of their political life in Munich in the early 1920s. Hitler and the Nazis meant many things to many men: in particular he appealed to the petty bourgeoisie, humiliated and angry in the aftermath of the lost war, who feared a Bolshevik-style revolution; Hitler drew on this fear and discontent, as he did on the disappointments of small industrialists, civil servants, workers and peasants. As late as 1932 Ernst Niekisch wrote of National Socialism that it 'floats, but no-one knows yet where. Every door is still open, none has been closed . . .' It was Niekisch's view that the 'National Socialist movement is ambiguous, with many meanings, various trends, emotions, ambitions and dreams embraced together as in a common bed . . . . It is full of contrasts; it contains as many contradictions as does the community of living people. It speaks with the voice of blood, but also with the voice of social revenge. The impulse of true national feeling is powerful; but it is shamelessly misused by personal pettiness and by calculating selfishness.' Its programme was all-embracing and ill-defined.

It took Hitler a long time — some twelve years — before he was able to prove himself. From its beginnings, his party was constructed on a broad social base. It was not a party based on class, for racial conflict, Hitler believed, would replace class

29

Communist and Nazi Working Classes, *Simplicissimus* February 1931 (far left)
This caricature, showing different groups of workers marching behind the red flag and the swastika, indicates the polarization of public opinion behind the two extremist parties.

Nazi Propaganda, Ente (left)
This cartoon, depicting Nazi 'gramophone records' mouthing the slogans 'Heil Hitler' and 'Down with Jewry', illustrates the nature and quality of early Nazi propaganda. From the very beginning the spoken rather than the written word was its chief instrument.

War of the Germans in Uniform, Karl Arnold, July 1932 (below left)
Another Arnold on civil violence: 'If it goes on like this, we'll only be left with the Salvation Army.'

Reportage, Herbert Marxen, *Jugend*, 1932 (below)
By 1932, para-military organizations transformed the streets of German towns into a battlefield. The familiar tragic accident is differently reported:
    One party newspaper: 'This regrettable car accident shows how important it is to look first left and then right when crossing the street.'
    Another party newspaper: 'Just at the point when our member was trying to take the revolver he accidentally found in a tram to a lost-property office . . .'
    An independent newspaper: 'Without wanting to take the side of one party or the other: one has to be careful when handling firearms.'

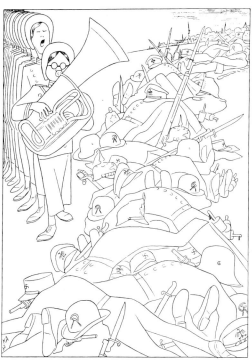

31

antagonism. White collar workers and civil
servants made up about 30 per cent of the early
membership; skilled and unskilled workers formed
almost the same proportion. About 16 per cent
were small tradesmen, most of the rest were
students, professional people and soldiers. Urban
outcasts and bohemians like Hitler himself made
up the ranks of the party activists and leaders; only
later they made a bid to win a following in the
countryside. Hitler said that 'For a
class-conscious worker there is no room in the
NSDAP, any more than there is for a
status-conscious bourgeois.'[1]

The magazine Niekisch had been publishing,
Widerstand (Resistance), closed down in 1934 and
Weber's work was confiscated. Niekisch and his
collaborators and friends were among those
persecuted when a wave of arrests swept over
Germany after the Reichstag fire on 27 February
1933. Niekisch himself was arrested, but was soon
freed from SA custody through the intervention of
his friends; he was rearrested in 1937 and released
in 1945. Weber spent most of 1937 in Gestapo
prisons in Hamburg, Berlin and Nuremberg; after
that, he went to Florida in 1938, returning to
Germany in 1939. He then started to work on two
cycles of lithographs, entitled Leviathan and
Reichtum aus Tränen (Riches from Tears) which
dealt with the exploitative nature of British
imperialism. The two cycles were published under

the title Britische Bilder (British Pictures) in 1941.
Such was the price Weber paid for his own survival
and that of his family under the Nazi regime. He
went on to serve in the army in the concluding
phase of the war.

Throughout his career, Weber's target was
broad and comprehensive. War profiteers, 'pullers
of strings', the 'chimney barons' (Schlotbarone)
the large industrialists after World War I; Hitler and
the National Socialist movement; British
imperialism. After World War II, he satirized the
mindless consumer society of the new Germany,
or the holidays from that society, taken by tourists
striving for vacuous perfectionism unattainable at
home.

Death often appeared in various guises in his
drawings. One deathly clown performed his stunt
before expectant masses on a ramp leading
nowhere, in Glanznummer (Star Turn). The drawing
Das Grauen also contained visual, as well as
verbal, indications of the coming disaster. Its
animal instinct allows the horse to sense the
coming horrors; Das Grauen is the dawn, but the
drawing and its title form an involved pun. Grau is
gray, and the frightened horse is that colour;
grauenhaft means 'gruesome', and that is the
future the animal stalls before. Drawings of the
kinds of animal who become metaphors for certain
types of human character or behaviour — as in a
fable — are probably the oldest form of pictorial

mockery; Weber also sometimes used the human-vegetable-animal blend to make his point. There are certain links between the work of Weber and of Hieronymus Bosch, especially with Bosch's *Garten der Lüste* (Garden of Pleasures); in his later work, after World War II, Weber used, perhaps unconsciously, symbolism similar to Bosch's.

In sharp contrast to Paul Weber's visionary work, Karl Arnold's cartoons had a lighter, humorous touch: he saw his target as an object of high comedy, rather than of doom. Like many of the best satirists who worked for *Simplicissimus* — Olaf Gulbransson was Norwegian, Karl Valentin came from Hesse-Saxony — Arnold was not Bavarian: he came from a state which no longer exists, the Duchy of Sachsen-Coburg-Gotha. Between the wars he worked for a number of German illustrated papers, and some of his earlier cartoons were banned by Hitler's regime, but after 1933 he ceased to produce work criticizing the regime.

His first drawing of a Nazi supporter dates from 1923: an inebriated Bavarian beer drinker calls at the same time for law and order, revolution (or is it revaluation?), *and* a pogrom against the Jews. Arnold was perhaps the first artist who used the swastika eyes motif; *The Race Person,* one of a gallery of 'New Types', drawn in the following year also for *Simplicissimus,* is altogether a better

PAUL WEBER was born in Arnstadt in Thuringia in 1893. His first lithographic attempts date from the years 1911–13 when, as a young man, he belonged to the romantic back-to-nature movement, the *Jung — Wandervögel.* He spent the first two years of World War I on the Russian front and contributed drawings and cartoons to the newspaper of the Tenth Army. For Weber, as for other German artists, the war was a formative experience. From then on a gloomy nightmarish quality never lifted from his work, which was dominated by the twin themes of death and material destruction. After his marriage in 1920 he began illustrating books and in 1925 founded the Clan-Presse, a printing company. Although a radical until about 1936, he then abandoned his outspoken resistance to the Nazi movement, probably worried about his family of five children. After spending most of 1937 in Gestapo prisons in Hamburg, Berlin and Nuremberg he went to Florida in the following year and returned to Germany in 1939 where he produced his lithographs attacking British imperialism.

A major exhibition of his work was held in Bonn and in Münster in 1978 on the occasion of his 85th birthday.

Book Burning, Bodo Gestenberg, May 1933
(above)
Gerstenberg's cartoon records the burning of
some 20,000 books in Berlin on 10 May 1933, 'a
scene', says William Shirer, 'which had not been
witnessed in the western world since the late
Middle Ages'. Any book was condemned to the
flames 'which acts subversively on our future or
strikes at the root of German thought, the
German home and the driving forces of our
people'. Among them were works by authors of
international reputation including Heinrich and
Thomas Mann, Stefan Zweig and Erich Maria
Remarque, and foreign writers such as H. G.
Wells, Gide, Zola and Proust.

He is a Writer, George Grosz, 1933 (right)
In this drawing Grosz depicts the SA searching
through the belongings of a terrified suspect; 'He
is a writer', they declare. Hitler's almost fanatical
hatred of intellectuals and the educated
middle-class (he called them 'rejects of nature')
can perhaps be traced to his own academic
failure and early rejection of intellectual
discipline. Grosz himself left Germany in 1933 as
did an estimated 2500 writers, either voluntarily
or under duress, constituting a 'diaspora unique
in history'.

Start 1932, Guppler, *Brennessel*, 30 December
1931 (opposite)
This pro-Nazi cartoon carries the legend: 'As for
the false reports of a National Socialist flying
corps: it is not we but the others who are taking
flight.' Drawn at the end of 1931, it shows an
exodus of communists and wealthy Jews, but
gives no hint of the mass flight of writers,
musicians and scientists — Thomas Mann,
Arnold Schoenberg, Kurt Weill, Albert Einstein
and thousands more — that was to ensue in the
next two years.

Zu den Falschmeldungen über das Nationalsozialistische Fliegerkorps:
Nicht wir fliegen — sondern die andern!

 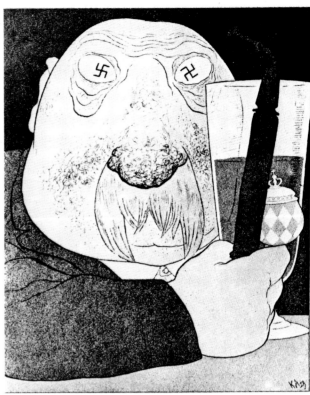

class of gentleman than his beer-cellar neighbour.

Paul Nikl's cartoon, *Furor Teutonicus,* in 1934, also belongs to the category of new types. Influenced by Grosz's style, it makes a sharp point about the kind of people who supported Hitler's movement. The central figure wears a *pince-nez* and a swastika brooch and is a lady of a forbidding aspect; her mean and gaunt, expectant expression and her hooded eyes look forward confidently to a bright Nazi future. The other National Socialist ladies are watchful, suspicious or bemused: it is a collection of clearly drawn, rather repulsive, symbols.

As long as the Nazi movement remained confined to its place of origin in Bavaria, the attack on it, in terms of caricature, also remained largely Bavarian; most of it appeared on the pages of *Simplicissimus.* After the National Socialist Party had spread its organization across the whole of Germany, the attack upon it broadened and began to appear elsewhere in Germany. George Grosz, Paul Weber, Karl Arnold and Theodor Heine saw Hitler and his movement from a close-up view. Their commentary on the Nazi phenomenon was incisive and, in Weber's case, prophetic. But they, in any case, preached to the converted, and it is impossible to describe their work as part of a broadly based campaign at any time before 1929. George Grosz wrote in later life: 'The time of the cartoon as an instrument in the struggle for

progress is over. If one wants to persecute nowadays, a photograph with a suitable text serves much better. Life and death are, if I may put it so, great themes for ridicule and cheap tricks.'[2] Grosz's friend John Heartfield, who invented the art of *photomontage,* used the photograph in this way to make his political points, adding a drawing, or editing several photographs together to produce the desired effect.

After its outbreak in August 1914, Heartfield abhorred the war, with its *Hurra-Patriotismus,* and started writing melancholy, pacifist poetry. Ernst Lissauer's loathsome but popular song of hate: 'We love united, we hate united, we have one enemy: England!' induced him to change his original name, Helmut Herzfelde, to the anglicized John Heartfield (Grosz anglicized his first name, Georg, for similar reasons). He kept his new name although the Reich authorities refused to register it during the war.

Heartfield's first political photomontage appeared on 15 February 1919 on the title page of the satirical magazine *Jedermann sein eigener Fussball* (Everybody His Own Football). It was entitled *Competition! Who is the Most Beautiful?* and it attacked Ebert's Social Democrat government. The magazine was banned after its first number but in the same year, Heartfield, his brother and George Grosz founded a new satirical magazine, *Die Pleite* (Bankruptcy).

Furor Teutonicus, Paul Nikl, 1934 (far left); *Hitler Supporter*, Karl Arnold, 1923 (centre), and *Upper Middle-Class Nazi Types*, Karl Arnold (left)
Although Hitler's supporters came from all social classes, one of Arnold's 'new types' is in fact the Nazi prototype. A Bavarian drunk, whose political thinking runs on the lines of irreconcilable opposites: 'We want to 'ave peace and also revaluation [revaluation and revolution are confused here], and there must be order and also a pogrom against the Jews. . . .'

For the next ten years or more Heartfield consistently attacked German politics, particularly National Socialism and allied phenomena in German life — Prussian militarism and the large-scale industries and industrialists who supplied it with arms. His picture entitled *After Ten Years: Fathers and Sons, 1924* was a strong argument against militarism and its leaders: in it a photograph of Hindenburg was set off by the skeletons of those he had led to death in 1914. *Hour of the Ghosts, 1930* puts the basic characters in the German drama into a ghostly setting. Hitler, with a confident smile, is waiting in the wings; on the opposite side, an old man in a formal dress with an Iron Cross is leaving the picture. The moonlit scene has a curious mobility about it, indicating that Hitler's own hour of ghosts was yet to come.

Throughout the 1920s and early 1930s, Heartfield assisted the Communist Party with its publicity work, and it was he who designed the last election poster for the party in March 1933. His flat was raided by the SA at Easter that year and a great part of his work was destroyed. He fled to Prague, where he worked for the re-established Malik Verlag and for the newspaper *AIZ (Arbeiter-Illustrierte-Zeitung)* — its name was changed to *Volks-Illustrierte* in the middle of 1936. His first photomontage for *AIZ* appeared in May 1933 and was called *Hitler's Programme.*

KARL ARNOLD, son of a puppet manufacturer, was born in 1883. He first attended design school in his birthplace Neustadt bei Coburg, where his teacher was Ernest Derra, and then in 1901 he went to the Academy of Arts in Munich where he attended Franz von Stuck's class, together with Vassily Kandinsky, Paul Klee, Hans Purrmann and Albert Weissgerber. His first contribution to *Simplicissimus* appeared in the twelfth volume, in 1907. He later became a regular contributor to the magazine and a leading satirical critic of the Weimar Republic; in 1913 he founded the *Neue Münchner Secession* with Bernard Blecker, Alexej von Jawlinsky and Paul Klee. After he joined the army in 1914, his drawings were published in the *Liller Kriegszeitung* and his war leaflets, *Kriegsflugblätter*, became popular in Germany.

He worked between the wars for a number of illustrated papers, and some of his earlier work was banned after the Nazis came to power. Much of his work was lost when his studio was destroyed in 1945. He died in 1953.

Heartfield's work was well represented in two Mannheim exhibitions in 1933, sponsored by the

Through Light into Night, 19 May 1933 (left); *Ten Years Later: Fathers and Sons,* 1924 (right) and *Hour of the Ghosts,* 1930 (below right); all by John Heartfield
In the powerful works of 1924 and 1930 Heartfield attacks the militarism he sees at the root of Germany's problems. 'Through light into night' was Heartfield's text accompanying a photomontage of Goebbels and the burning of the books.

new Nazi regime, and entitled 'Horror Chamber of Art' and *Kulturbolschewismus.* Hitler lost no time in revenging himself on 'decadent' artists.

Heartfield exhibited in Prague in 1934, in Paris in 1935, and in New York in 1938; in 1936, there was a room devoted to Heartfield's work at the International Photograph Exhibition at Mánes in Prague; the German Minister protested, and some of Heartfield's work was confiscated by the police. In the same year, the first monograph on Heartfield by Sergei Tretiakov appeared in Moscow. In 1938 the Czechoslovak government refused to extradite Heartfield to Germany; helped by Ernest Hemingway's wife, the journalist Martha Gellhorn, and the English reporter Eric Gedye Heartfield left Prague for London. After the German occupation of post-Munich Czechoslovakia in March 1939, five boxes containing Heartfield's work were thrown into the river Vltava. In December 1939, an exhibition of his surviving work, 'One Man's War against Hitler' took place at the Arcade Gallery in London, but in 1940 Heartfield was interned in enemy alien camps, and only released because of a serious illness and an intervention in the House of Commons. He spent five years in London, working as a freelance designer for several publishers, including Allen Lane's Penguin books, before settling in East Germany, where he died in 1968.

Heartfield's work was highly innovative,

provocative and controversial. It harnessed photography for political purposes: his designs for book-jackets used a similar technique. Modern advertising methods informed his work, and he relied on the sharpest contrast, the maximum shock and the broadest appeal.

Heartfield and Grosz had first experimented with photograph collages in 1915; Heartfield later said that his pencil could no longer adequately describe and attack the war he so much abhorred. A similar view — that conventional artistic media no longer sufficed to bear witness to the twentieth century — had been expressed, as early as 1912, by Kurt Tucholsky: 'We need many more photographs. No agitation can be conducted more effectively . . . Nothing proves more, nothing excites more than these pictures . . . with contrast and juxtaposition. And with little text.'[3] Heartfield was the first artist who understood, and was excited by, the possibilities opened up by contrasting two or more photographs. A new reality emerged when heterogeneous photographic material was used which threw a sharp, unusual light on the everyday life of society.

**NACH
ZEHN JAHREN:
VÄTER UND SÖHNE
1924**

GESPENSTERSTUNDE 1930

The Burden of the Swastika, David Low, *Evening Standard*, 29 June 1933

The Destruction of the Weimar Republic

Those unfortunate peoples in Central Europe who had lost too many battles, or who never fought them and then looked back on a past of unfulfilled promises or alien rule, have a myth of an army eternally asleep in a vast cave in a mountain. It will, in a moment of supreme national crisis, be woken by a charismatic leader and come to the rescue of the long-suffering people. In German folklore, there exists the figure of such a leader; and of an army dozing in the bowels of a mountain. There was a connection between Hitler, his movement, and this myth. All fascist leaders were presented as men who had thought deeply and wisely about the misfortunes of their people — and who had the desired remedy. Hitler's party was a party of crisis. In 1923, when he first sought political power in Munch, the French had occupied the Rhineland. After the failed November *putsch,* Hitler was sent to prison, where he wrote *Mein Kampf.* The book includes a reflection on the misfortunes of his people and his proposals for remedying them. After his release, he set about reorganizing the party, purging it of all the democratic elements of its early period and giving it a tight, authoritarian character under a single leader, himself. Yet by 1928 the party had only 60,000 members and in the Reich elections of the same year gained only twelve seats — less than half its goal. Hitler's chance came, by luck, in 1929. The problem of reparations came up again that year, coinciding with the world-wide economic depression.

Alfred Hugenberg, an unscrupulous old man, one of the 'grey, moth-eaten eagles' in Nazi terminology and since 1928 the leader of the extreme right *Deutschnationale Volkspartei,* believed he could make use of a gifted agitator like Adolf Hitler. Hugenberg controlled a vast press and film empire and did much to put an end to the process of conciliation between the right and the Weimar Republic. Hitler was coaxed into an alliance with Hugenberg on condition that he would remain independent in propaganda and retain a good share of the funds on offer. Gregor Strasser, whose anti-capitalist views were well known, became Hitler's representative on the joint financing committee. With the support of Hugenberg's vast organization, Hitler quickly achieved the nationwide publicity he had previously sought in vain, but Hugenberg foolishly still believed that he could use his new ally for his own ends.

Hitler's marginal, extremist party, at that time more an object of ridicule than of awe, gained access not only to funds but to well-disposed mass media as well. They were used by the party's effective and cunning propaganda apparatus for an assault on a broad front against the constitutional nature of the Weimar Republic. Hitler soon became a national political figure with enough time

to spare to formalize the party's symbols and decorations. He could now afford to buy a palace for the party headquarters in Munich; he spent much time with the architect planning and designing the interior decoration. The Barlow Palace was then renamed the 'Brown House', after Hitler's favourite colour, the colour of the SA uniforms. His own office contained a bust of Mussolini, a portrait of Frederick the Great and a painting of an attack by Hitler's own regiment in Flanders during a World War I offensive. There was a Führer chair in the canteen in the cellar of the Brown House.

In February 1930, after he had broken with Hugenberg's conservative allies, Hitler said that the victory of the National Socialist movement would take three years at the most. In March the party published an agrarian programme, which complimented the 'noblest class of the nation' and promised it generous subsidies for its produce. In September 1930 the number of unemployed stood at over three million; in January 1932 more than six million unemployed were registered: about every second family in the country was directly affected. Hitler ruthlessly exploited the economic situation, blaming capitalism, communism, the Jews, the Weimar democracy. The Republic started to show signs of disintegration: the coalition government broke up in the spring of 1930, and there was a flight by almost all political parties into opposition.

Hitler's NSDAP, the most organized, the most clamorous and the most consistent party of opposition, offered refuge to everyone who felt the need of it, regardless of class, age, or motives. The 'sinking middle class' — office workers, tradesmen and small industrialists — and the peasants sought refuge in the party. Hitler, recognizing that this was his hour to strike, now used his extraordinary demagogic talent to the full to win over massive sections of the population.

The depression also made it possible for the Nazis to score their first successes among industrial workers on a national basis. The embattled Nazi social-revolutionary left, led by Gregor Strasser, made its last bid to stop the party from becoming mainly a collection of lower-middle class anti-semites but there were also signs — especially when he broke with Hugenberg — that Hitler himself was taking a left turn. Karl Arnold's drawing in *Simplicissimus* made that point in his cartoon entitled *Hitler, the National Marxist,* in which the ghost of Karl Marx asks Hitler to return his theories to the socialists. Where the party failed, the SA did better. It proved to be a good home for the unemployed who in Hamburg, for instance, made up 60 per cent of SA strength. While the ranks of the SA grew, it came into increasingly sharp clashes with the communists who felt themselves threatened on their own working-class territory.

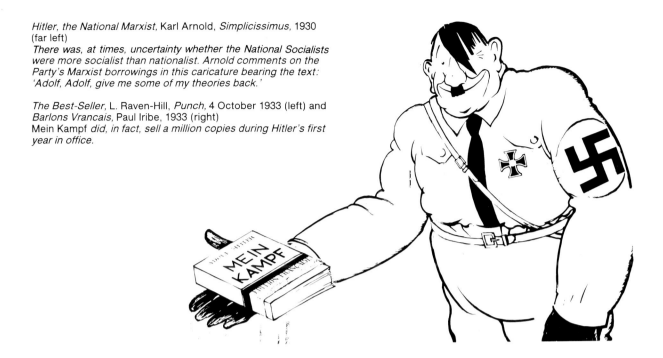

Hitler, the National Marxist, Karl Arnold, *Simplicissimus*, 1930
(far left)
There was, at times, uncertainty whether the National Socialists
were more socialist than nationalist. Arnold comments on the
Party's Marxist borrowings in this caricature bearing the text:
'Adolf, Adolf, give me some of my theories back.'

The Best-Seller, L. Raven-Hill, *Punch*, 4 October 1933 (left) and
Barlons Vrancais, Paul Iribe, 1933 (right)
Mein Kampf did, in fact, sell a million copies during Hitler's first
year in office.

The election in September 1930 indicated that the end was near for the government of the Weimar Republic by the democratic parties and brought Hitler closer to power. His party increased its vote from the 810,000 of two years earlier to 6.4 million. It was the second largest party, after the Social Democrats, in the Reichstag, with 107 members, and it was committed to destroying the system by which it was elected. There was no longer any question of a socialist commitment from Hitler and his party. The Strasser crisis earlier in the election year meant a decisive defeat of the social-revolutionary wing of the party: when Otto Strasser declared, on 4 July, that he was leaving the party, no-one followed him. Under the title *Six Million Nazi Voters: Food for a Big Mouth*, John Heartfield showed the little fish, 'with God for Hitler and capital', being swallowed by the big fish of capitalism and Nazism. In another photomontage Heartfield predicted the death of parliament: big capital, the church and the Nazi party symbols on the chairman's seat dominated the empty chamber. There was a double pun in the drawing, and its text: 'That remains from the year 1848! The Reichstag will look like this when it opens on 13 October 1930.' The failure of the 1848 revolutionary parliament in Frankfurt was invoked, as well as paragraph 48 of the Weimar constitution, which gave the President of the Republic emergency powers. Kurt Tucholsky, the satirist,

said about Hitler at that time: 'The man does not exist, he is only the noise he makes.' In one of the early anti-Nazi cartoons to appear in England, David Low, in the *Evening Standard,* linked a child-size Hitler with the Wilhelmine imperial tradition; he showed off his tricks, including an imperial moustache, before amazed parents.

Though the uncertainty about the National Socialist party's 'socialist' leanings had been settled, Hitler and his movement, now vastly successful, appeared more complex in a close-up, local German view. Only the sources of Hitler's support were picked out by the cartoonists with a sure touch: his intentions, and his ruthless determination, less so. In 1932 after Hitler had addressed the Industries Club, a cartoon in the Social Democrat daily, *Vorwärts* (p. 49) saw him as a tool of big capital: the manipulated puppet was still pretending to fight capitalism. John Heartfield made a similar point more strongly, without the implication that Hitler was necessarily being manipulated: his words that 'millions stand behind me' were used in the photomontage entitled *The Meaning of the Hitler Salute.*

Willi Geiger picked on Hitler's demagogic political style, as well as on his preoccupation with youth, in the drawing *Suffer the Little Children to Come unto Me!* Hitler's party, as well as the SA, were young. In the year 1931, some 70 per cent of the SA troopers in Berlin were under thirty and

A Breakdown: A Pleasing Phenomenon!, Oskar Garvens, 1932 (right)
Garvens comments on the profusion of parliamentary parties in Weimar Germany; none could alone maintain a majority in the Reichstag, and parliamentary democracy became unworkable. In the centre of the wheel, Michael, the long-suffering prototype of the German people, has lost interest in the proceedings.

David Low, *Little Adolf Tries on the Spiked Moustache* Evening Standard, *1930 (below).*
In his early cartoons, Low could not take Hitler seriously.

Hitler
LITTLE ADOLF TRIES ON THE SPIKED MOUSTACHE

'Suffer the Little Children to
Come unto Me!'
Willi Geiger (left)
Hitler's obsession with the
young is given an embarrassing
Christian analogy.

Principles of German
Education, Josef Čapek,
14 May 1933 (above)
Education in the Third Reich, as
Hitler saw it, was to be a
Spartan military and political
training culminating in service
in the armed forces. Čapek
quotes Wilhelm Frick, Hitler's
Minister of the Interior: 'The
German school must create a
political individual. We must and
will endow our youth with a
national consciousness.'

DAS BLIEB VOM JAHRE 18**48** ÜBRIG!

Ich
führe Euch herrlichen Pleiten entgegen!

almost 40 per cent of the total membership of the party belonged to that age group. Some 60 per cent of Nazi deputies to the Reichstag were less than forty years old; in contrast, only 10 per cent of the Social Democrat deputies were under forty. Hitler was only forty-one at the time of the 1930 elections; Karl Kaufmann became a party *Gauleiter* at twenty-five, Goebbels at twenty-eight. Himmler was the same age when he was appointed the *Reichsführer* of the SS — the *Schutzstaffel*, originally Hitler's personal bodyguard. Baldur von Schirach became the Nazi youth leader at twenty-six.[1]

The dynamism and the sheer physical energy of the party were beyond question, but there was still uncertainty on where the Nazi party was going. Hitler threatened the Weimar Republic in one speech and then swore loyalty to it in the next; he offered an alliance to the men who guarded the gate on the way to power — Hindenburg and the army — only to turn to attack them and tell them firmly to meet him half-way. There was much tactical calculation in Hitler's sudden switches of policy; but underneath cold calculation, there was an infirmity of purpose, a flaw in Hitler's character. He was indecisive: he took risks without working out their likely short- and medium-term outcome. He preferred to skip that stage and quickly move on to the last options open to him: either a *putsch*, or abandoning politics altogether.

Instead of consistently attacking the Weimar Republic, Hitler chose the devious and politically easier and more profitable way of undermining the Weimar system by an assault on the political parties, the Social Democrats and the Communists in particular. He had succeeded in making the fragmented right more coherent but the full force of his attack was concentrated on the 'Marxists'. In the last two years or so of the Republic's existence, he managed to literally transform the streets of Germany into a battleground; he said that while electoral victory was the concern of the bourgeois parties there was much more at stake for the Nazis. 'We recognize quite clearly that if Marxism wins, we will be annihilated. Nor would we expect anything else. But if we win, Marxism will be annihilated, and totally.'[2]

On 13 March 1932 Hitler was a candidate in the presidential election; Hindenburg defeated him but fell short of absolute majority. Hindenburg was re-elected President of the Republic in April with Social Democrat support, though the votes cast for Hitler increased. In the Reichstag elections on 31 July 1932 the Nazis more than doubled their former number of seats to 230, still without commanding a majority in the parliament. Before the elections, the SA and the SS had been banned: a severe blow to the party, which Hitler decided not to challenge. In the meanwhile, Hindenburg dismissed Chancellor Brüning and

The Defunct Parliament, John Heartfield, 8 October 1930 (far left)
The picture contains a double pun: a reference to the parliament of Frankfurt of 1848, and to paragraph 48 of the Weimar constitution, which gave the President of the Republic emergency powers. Heartfield's original text read: 'That remains from the year 1848! The Reichstag *will look like this when it opens on 13 October 1930.'*

His Majesty Adolf, John Heartfield, 24 August 1932 (left)
Flushed with victory after the elections of July 1932, Hitler now demanded the chancellorship of the Republic. Heartfield saw this as the culmination of his ambitions and a return to the authoritarian rule of imperial Germany. The ironic legend 'I lead you toward magnificent disasters!' is a play on the words of Kaiser Wilhelm's boast: 'I lead you toward a magnificent era.' ('Pleiten' instead of 'Zeiten'.)

'Millions Stand Behind Me' — The Meaning of the Hitler Greeting, John Heartfield, 16 October 1932 (right)
Heartfield shows Hitler's dependence on capitalist sources of funds, without in any way indicating his subservience to his benefactors.

MILLIONEN
stehen hinter mir

DER SINN DES HITLERGRUSSES

appointed von Papen to succeed him. There was an easy-going, cavalier quality about von Papen: he was expelled in 1916 from Washington, where he was serving as military attaché, for attempted sabotage, and then managed to mislay his secret documents so that they fell into the hands of the British. But von Papen was well-connected and expected to be able to form a coalition government. Having no political base or experience, von Papen formed a 'cabinet of barons'. There were seven noblemen in the government, two company directors, a general and a former patron of Hitler. Neither the middle nor the working class was represented in the select group.

Oskar Garvens (1874–1951), the sculptor and painter who was a regular contributor to the satirical newspaper *Kladderadatsch,* commented on the 'parliamentary madhouse' in 1932 in the cartoon (p. 44) entitled *A Breakdown: A Pleasing Phenomenon!* The German Michael — the simple, long-suffering prototype of the people, the equivalent of John Bull or Uncle Sam — at the centre of the fairground wheel, the parliamentary wheel of fortune, had given up turning it, and the Nazis were stuck at the top to their amazement and joy. Michael also appeared in Karl Arnold's drawings, when Arnold returned to mocking the Nazis in the last phase of the Weimar Republic. The Nazi slogan 'Germany Awake!' was the title of

his drawing (p. 50) with the text 'Unnecessary noise, young people! I have not slept since 1914.' Freedom of choice, crippled by political indecision, dominated Arnold's cartoons, as it did the political situation in Germany at the time. In another of his cartoons (p. 51) the girl Germania cannot decide which political hat to wear. In yet another of his drawings, Michael, who is very poor, says to the beautiful temptresses offering him crowns of several political kinds: 'Many thanks for your offer, my ladies, but at present I have no shirt to wear.' Hitler's own uncertain role was expressed in a cartoon by Thomas Theodor Heine (p. 51) where he is being consoled at the time of the presidential elections in 1932: 'Don't worry about that, Adolf. Being ridiculous is not fatal in Germany. If you could not become a police inspector you can always try to be the Reich President.' Hitler's ambition was also recorded in John Heartfield's picture entitled *His Majesty Adolf* with the text 'I lead you toward magnificent disasters!' Karl Arnold showed Hitler in three roles, in the drawing of 1932 entitled *Let Us Build Monuments* (p. 52). The Karolinenplatz in Munich, near the scene of Hitler's failed *putsch* in November 1923, is decorated with a statue of Hitler as the 'Well-known soldier' in a reference to the war memorials to the Unknown Soldier; he poses as the dancer Salome, pinching the Jewish nose of a severed head; he is also a robot drummer who

National Socialists and Capitalists, Vorwärts, 1932 (right) and
SOS German Nationalists, Karl Arnold, December 1929 (far
right)
The drawing in the Social Democratic Party newspaper
*Vorwärts points out that the Nazis' so-called workers' party was
backed by big capital. Entitled 'No-one plays with the Party's
fire unscathed', Arnold's cartoon shows the Nationalist leader
Hugenberg trying to escape from his damaging alliance with the
Nazis, while its intended target, the Communist Party, remains
unharmed. The Nationalists were to lose heavily in the following
year's elections, while both Nazis and communists gained
seats.*

The German Way of the Cross, Paul Thessig, (below)
*Paul Thessig takes up the same theme as Low did (p. 40) in this
less powerful drawing of an aged man who is also half beast of
burden carrying a cross. Few Germans, however, thought of
their future in this way. Hitler's seizure of power had been legal
and was, as he himself claimed, 'one of the most bloodless
revolutions in world history.'*

48

plays the 'National-Marseillaise' when a coin is inserted into the machine, which Jews are forbidden to operate.

Von Papen, of whom much had been expected, in the end pleased no-one. At a meeting with von Papen on 18 January 1933 Hitler demanded the Chancellorship for himself. In *The Boss on His Travels* Arnold commented on the relationship between the two men, with the other parties looking on: 'A card will be enough, I shall be back straightaway.' Hitler was back, as the new Chancellor, on 30 January 1933. He came in through the back door, accepting a cabinet which was intended to contain him, to box him in. (Von Papen had arrogantly dismissed warnings about Hitler with the words, 'You're wrong; we've hired him.') There were three National Socialist ministers in the new government against eight conservatives. But the latter were in the government and in politics in order to defend the traditional privileges of their class rather than political values which would have kept Hitler in his place. Oswald Spengler, the German pessimist historian, said that there was no victory because there were no opponents. He added, in a rare flash of optimism:

The national revolution of 1933 was something powerful and it will remain so in the eye of the future, through the elemental impersonal force, with which it was accomplished. That was Prussian through and through,

as was the departure of 1914, which changed souls in a moment. Germany's dreamers raised themselves, peacefully, with imposing ease, and opened a way to the future.[3]

Spengler's view was not generally shared. Paul Thessig saw the Germans as carrying a new kind of cross (p. 48); the same point was made, in graphic terms, more strongly in David Low's *Evening Standard* cartoon which appeared on 29 June 1933. A few months before Hitler came to power Karl Arnold's *Simplicissimus* title-page (May 1932) cartoon (p. 52) contained a broad hint on the kind of regime Hitler was likely to establish. The shadow of Frederick the Great behind a grim Hitler, the text inverting the King of Prussia's famous words, 'In my state everyone will find salvation in his own way' to Hitler's 'In my state everyone will find salvation in my own way.' Straightaway, Hitler used his private army and its pre-war 1933 terrorist tactics to underpin his power and intimidate his opponents. Some of their criminal activities were punished by legal action, but by no means all of them. The Czech cartoonist Bidlo showed the criminal nature of Hitler's regime and of the SA thugs in several cartoons (pp. 22, 52). Popular enthusiasm was not what it seemed to be.

Only five days after Hitler's accession to power a decree 'for the protection of the German people' was published. Political meetings as well as

newspapers of rival parties could be banned for the vaguest of reasons. The *Geheime Staatspolizei,* the Gestapo, was established and the communists became its first and chief target. The legal revolution was on the way. The Reichstag fire on 27 February gave it an additional impetus: it would have been completed anyway. The same night some 4,000 people were arrested: communists, writers, doctors, lawyers. The following day, Hitler put a new emergency decree before President Hindenburg. It abolished civil rights, including *habeas corpus,* extended the death penalty to a new list of offences and strengthened the position of the central Reich government with regard to the states. The men who were supposed to contain Hitler in the cabinet, including von Papen, made the completion of the Nazi revolution possible. Constitutional government was replaced by a permanent state of emergency.

Nevertheless, in the last multi-party elections before the end of World War II, on 5 March 1933, Hitler's Nazis did not achieve the success he had hoped for. They missed the majority in the Reichstag by nearly forty seats. They won 288 seats and only by adding the 52 seats of their Nationalist Coalition partners did they achieve a marginal majority; the Centre party kept its 73 seats and the Social Democrats 120. The Communists still held 100 seats, losing only 19.

Yet Hitler retaliated by declaring in the cabinet that the election was a revolution, and in the four days starting on 7 March the Nazis seized control in the German states in a series of virtual *coups d'état.* On the day the new Reichstag was to open, 21 March, Hitler and his Propaganda Minister, Goebbels, staged an impressive ceremony which attempted to reconcile the new Germany with the old. Hindenburg and Hitler shook hands on the steps of the Garrison Church in Potsdam; the symbol of national reconciliation appeared in millions of newspaper copies and posters. Hitler said that, without the old gentleman's blessing, he would not have wanted to take power. The final destruction of the relics of Weimar democracy could now be completed with ease.

THOMAS THEODOR HEINE, the co-founder of the satirical magazine *Simplicissimus,* was born in 1867. Heine was the artist most intimately connected with the magazine's fortunes and influenced both its artistic and political content. During his years with the magazine he executed more than 2500 drawings. He left Hitler's Germany, first for Prague and then for Sweden where he died in 1948. He wrote an autobiographical novel *I Am Waiting for Miracles (Ich Warte auf Wunder),* published in Stockholm in 1945.

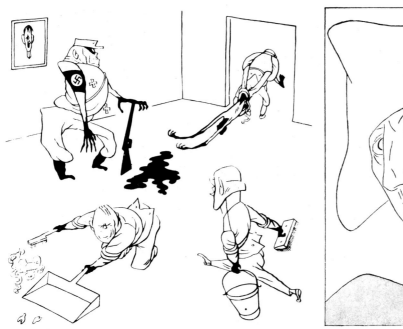

Germany, The Tidiest Country in the World,
František Bidlo (above)
In the early years of the Third Reich, the
diminishing minority who opposed the regime
were swiftly and silently dealt with, as Bidlo's
cartoon shows.

Hail Prussian!, Karl Arnold, Simplicissimus,
May 1932 (above right), and Let Us Build
Monuments, Karl Arnold, 1932 (right)
Arnold alludes to the notion that Hitler was
the successor to Frederick the Great. Hitler
declares: 'In my state everyone will find
salvation in my way', an inversion of
Frederick's statement advocating religious
freedom: 'In my state everyone will find
salvation in his own way.' Arnold shows some
suitable monuments to Hitler; as the
well-known soldier, as Salome and as a
mechanical drummer.

Principles of Nazi Education, Part II, Josef Čapek, 14 May 1933 (left)
Čapek continues his comments on the links between Nazi education and violence in this caricature. The legend is another quotation from Frick: 'The great experience of the collapse of the liberal-Marxist world conception and the victorious triumph of National Socialist thought must become the basic part of the study of history.'

Popular Enthusiasm, Fulk (below left)
The real nature of popular enthusiasm for the Nazi party.

53

You Will Laugh — I Know Nothing About It, Bodo Gerstenberg, 1945
A late view of Göring, referring to his naive belief at the end of the war that he could negotiate with the Allies, disclaiming all knowledge of Nazi atrocities.

The Leaders of the New Germany

Hitler's position in the party and in the state was unchallengeable. He may have occasionally hesitated when several courses of action were open to him, but he was ruthlessly determined in his pursuit of power. He saw politics and life in terms of crude power relationships: propaganda, for him a key political activity, aimed to achieve 'an encroachment upon man's freedom of will'. He saw human relations almost exclusively in terms of a hierarchy: who could give orders to whom. Hitler was quite unable to grasp the rights of others or their claim to happiness. If he had any feelings of affection or compassion, he managed effectively to suppress them. He promoted, demoted and juggled people. He was a cold manipulator and the path of his advance was littered with bodies. But he rose with the help of others who were suitably rewarded for their efforts on his behalf.

Ernst Röhm was one of Hitler's closest assistants, who perhaps did more for the party and its leader than anyone else. A strong man with a florid, bullet-scarred face, he was a superb organizer, but by temperament a fighter. He was as loyal to his friends — and he had a close, sentimental attachment to Hitler — as Hitler was faithless. He divided the human race simply into civilians and soldiers, enemies and friends. He was frank and direct, a tough homosexual who had no conscience. Hitler's oratory in the early days in Munich impressed him and he joined the Nazi

Party as member number 623. He then held the rank of a captain as political advisor on the staff of General von Epp, his wartime commanding officer and now head of the SA's Office of Defence Policy. Röhm was thus in a position to render the infant party with many necessities including arms, funds and recruits. Röhm's men brought into the party a tough military swagger and more than a hint of violence. However, after the failure of the November 1923 *putsch*, Hitler broke with him; he was hard to fit into the new conception of the party, in which the SA — the *Sturmabteilung*, the Nazi paramilitary organization commanded by Röhm — was to be subordinated to the political organization. From 1925 the SA was led by Franz Pfeffer von Salomon whose task was, in Hitler's words, to train the SA 'not according to military principles but according to the needs of the party'. Röhm meanwhile withdrew from political life and went to Bolivia as a military instructor. Pfeffer carried out his orders faithfully but rivalries within the SA and Pfeffer's lack of personal self-confidence meant that in the autuman of 1930 he was forced to resign and Hitler took over as the supreme leader of the SA. He recalled Röhm from Bolivia to take over the day-to-day running of the SA as its chief of staff. By the end of 1932, it had 2.5 million men.

Hitler's moves after Röhm's return were in character. Hitler's authority within the Party and

The Berlin Gang, Boris
Efimov, (right)
*From right to left, Rosenberg,
Ley drunk, Ribbentrop,
Himmler, and Goebbels, as
close to Hitler as he can get,
Hess anonymous, Göring fat.
It seems that the implication
of the cartoon is that only
other Germans could take
that lot seriously.*

Supreme Obscurantist, Boris
Efimov, 1942 (below right)
*Efimov depicts Alfred
Rosenberg as a Nordic
warrior dancing around a
bonfire made up of books by
Heine, Shakespeare, Darwin
and others and carrying in
one hand a book on racial
theory and in the other a
totem pole of the cult of the
god Wotan.*

Old Iron . . . Old Lumber,
Stephen Roth, (below)
*A much-decorated fighter
pilot in World War I, Göring
had once been called 'the
Iron man', an image he tried
hard to live up to. Roth
satirizes it by showing him
covered with the medals and
decorations he loved while
puffing on an expensive cigar,
a symbol of the good living he
indulged in. In the street a
Japanese scrap-metal
collector covetously eyes the
'old iron' on Göring's chest.*

Beginning of the End — A German Hero's Death, Eric Godal, 1934 (left).
This caricature depicting the death of Röhm clearly hints at his homosexual excesses and carries the ironic legend: 'Fallen on the field of honour.'

If Röhm Were to Marry, Bidlo, (below left) *Röhm's homosexual proclivities were well-known. This cartoon shows Röhm with a fictional bride — followed down the aisle by his simpering and sorrowing 'best man' and SA guards.*

57

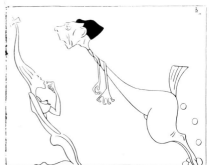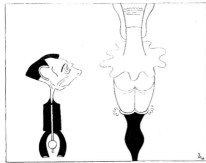

'My haunches no longer hide a thoroughbred . . . I am carried like a floating island . . . Towards freedom.'
'My feet are firmly placed on the earth of my home country. I am surrounded by the smell of the soil. The blood of a peasant rises slowly and healthily in me . . . .'
'Everything stood still in me, like the tied-down pendulum of a clock.'
Michael, František Bidlo, 1931
This strip cartoon is based on quotations from Goebbels' only novel, of the same name.

out of it was, of course, greater than in 1923, and Röhm's ways suited the political situation in the last two or three years before Hitler came to power. Nevertheless, Hitler began to build up the SS, which in 1929 accounted for only 480 men, into an elite police force within the Party. In the SA, Röhm replaced Pfeffer's officers with his own, largely homosexual friends, and after January 1933 his own brown army was free to hunt, torture and murder on an unprecedented scale (in the first nine months of the regime some 500 or 600 people were murdered and about 100,000 were sent to concentration camps). After January 1933 most of Hitler's leading lieutenants, Goebbels, Göring, Himmler and Hess, consolidated their power by acquiring state functions, but Röhm went his own way. He revived the SA's old militaristic ideals and organized impressive parades throughout the country. He continued building up its membership, to some 3.5 to 4 million men. He also tried to gain hold over the administration of the states and over publishing, but his chief objective was to absorb the smaller *Reichswehr* into his vast army. To this end he intensified the SA training programme and bought arms abroad, while criticising the regime, its foreign policy and other Nazi leaders.

It got to the point that neither Hitler nor the *Reichswehr* generals could tolerate Röhm's ambitions any longer. As early as June 1933 Hitler's government began breaking up SA camps

for protective custody and the SA police squads were disbanded. Discontent and talk of a 'second revolution' spread through Röhm's men: they felt that they had done much for the revolution and that the regime now overlooked their merits. Röhm naively told a friend 'Adolf is rotten. He goes around with reactionaries. His old comrades are not good enough for him. So he brings in these East Prussian generals.'[1] In his dull-witted way, he simply did not understand Hitler's tactical moves. On 17 April 1934 Röhm appeared in public with Hitler for the last time at a concert given by the SS in Berlin. Early in June 1934 the SS and the *Sicherheitsdienst,* the security service, were ordered to keep a close watch on the SA. On 26 June Hitler telephoned Röhm and summoned him and other SA leaders for discussion at Bad Wiessee. Four days later Röhm and other SA leaders were arrested and killed. Röhm paid the price for his ambition, as well as for his closeness to Hitler over many years.

The SA was a more frequent, and perhaps more suitable, target for mockery than Röhm. Perhaps the most appropriate portrait of Ernst Röhm deals with his fictitious wedding, condoned but regretted by his intimates in the SA. In London David Low commented on the way Hitler dealt with Röhm in a drawing in which the SA saluted Hitler with both arms (p. 60). The end of Röhm and of his organization was described in the drawing on the

Fascist Lie Gun, Kukriniksy, 1942 (above left) and *Goebbels and Hitler,* Fulk (above right)
Hitler used Goebbels, and Goebbels enjoyed being used: the Soviet three-man team of caricaturists, Kukriniksy, implied that there was a certain relentless and competitive quality about Goebbels. Goebbels likes opening his mouth wide and so does Fulk's baby. Hitler is convinced that it is Goebbels' child. In fact, Hitler did take a close interest in Goebbels' family affairs.

proverbial, mythical loyalty of the Germans: 'There is no death in the world more beautiful than to be killed by a friend.' (See Introduction, page 14.) Subsequently, the demise of the SA causes a crisis in hell (p. 61).

Josef Goebbels' relationship with Hitler was also uneven, though Goebbels was the only one of the Nazi leaders who remained with Hitler till the end in the embattled bunker in Berlin in April 1945. As a recent graduate in philology Goebbels wrote to Hitler, in prison in 1924, that what Hitler had said at his trial was 'the catechism of a new political creed coming to birth in the midst of a collapsing, secularized world'. Goebbels, who was a Rhinelander, originally worked in the 'West region of the Nazi Party, and believed that there was room inside the party for a socialist alternative to Hitler's south German fascism. After a meeting in Bamberg in February 1926 Goebbels wrote incredulously in his diary: 'I feel stunned. What is Hitler? A reactionary? Incredibly clumsy and insecure. Russian question: completely beside the point. Italy and England our natural allies: sensible! Our task is smashing Bolshevism. Bolshevism is a Jewish plot! We must inherit Russia! 180 million people!!!'[2] Nor was Goebbels convinced, at the time, that the key article of faith in Hitler's catechism, that the capitalist and Bolshevik Jew were the same, was quite correct.

Small and wiry with a club foot, Goebbels was,

as a demagogic orator, in a class near Hitler's. His approach to the audience was cool and calculated, and he was perhaps the most intelligent among the Nazi leaders. He swung over to Hitler's camp well before Hitler's conflict with the Strasser brothers and did much useful work for the movement in Berlin in the late 1920s. His interest and skill in propaganda and publicity work created a special bond with Hitler, though the strength of this bond was not always constant. Very important as propaganda was for Hitler before 1933, its comparative value declined as he acquired other means of exerting political influence. In addition, shortly before the outbreak of the war, Goebbels was involved in a scandal in which Hitler was forced to intervene (he planned to leave his wife and family for an actress who was Czech, and therefore a member of an inferior race). Although this temporarily diminished Goebbels' standing he was given an opportunity to prove his endurance and loyalty to Hitler during the war. Minister of Propaganda and Public Enlightenment since 1933, Goebbels urged the German people to endure the last, unbearable phase of the war longer than they might have done without his encouragement.

As a young man Goebbels had written a rather bad novel. Its publication in 1931 gave František Bidlo, the Czech cartoonist, the opportunity to draw a character sketch of Goebbels: his strip cartoon laid bare Goebbels' pretensions (p. 58).

Hitler   Göbbels   Göring

THEY SALUTE WITH BOTH HANDS NOW

'Will the Audience Kindly Keep Their Seats', Bert Strube, *Daily Express,* 3 July 1934 (left); *They Salute With Both Hands Now,* David Low, *Evening Standard,* 3 July 1934 (below left); *The Devils' Revolt,* Eric Godal (right), and *Night of the Long Knives,* Josef Flatters, 1939 (below right)

These cartoons refer to the 'blood purges' of 30 June 1934 which marked the elimination of Röhm and the SA who were accused of plotting armed rebellion against the state. More than 1000 'traitors' and others were summarily and arbitrarily killed in this bloody massacre, out of the 170,000 members Röhm had built up. In Godal's cartoon even the devils are frightened of them, calling: 'Every man for himself. Here come the SA.'

The Flatters drawing points a Wagnerian parallel — the murder of the heroic Siegfried by Hagen in Götterdämmerung.

The Jews are Our Guests and They Will be Treated Accordingly, František Bidlo
Bidlo points to the discrepancy between Goebbels' words and actions.

The Constitution of the German Reich, Karl Arnold, *Simplicissimus* 12 March 1933
The caption reads: 'The German Reich is a republic. Power stems from the people . . .'

Goebbels was preoccupied with sex, but found it hard to fit adequate words to his overpowering feelings. He was influenced by the cheap philosophy of the German *völkisch* — populist — philosophers of the nineteenth century, and by the various racist nonsense in circulation at the time. The basic link between blood and soil — *Blut und Boden,* or *Blubo* in popular parlance — was often the starting point of such flights of fancy. Goebbels took a self-confident, complacent view of women and of their roles; he was a tremendous optimist, though the objectives of his optimism were ill-defined; and he began taking an interest in the Jews.

František Bidlo contrasted Goebbels' relatively mild pronouncements about the Jews with the way they were actually treated.

Where Goebbels had wit and intelligence to offer to the movement, Hermann Göring added class to it and a certain flawed glamour. Before the end of the Great War, Captain Göring commanded the legendary Richthofen fighter squadron. A sturdy, easy-going man with a loud voice, he joined the party in its early days in Munich, but had little interest in the assorted Nazi ideological baggage. He travelled more than the other Nazi leaders, had an attractive Swedish wife and good connections but there was a certain predatory air about him. In 1933 Göring's vanity was satisfied by the office of a Minister without Portfolio; he also controlled the Prussian police as the Minister of the Interior in Prussia. His fatness and his jovial ways scarcely concealed Göring's brutal methods in the process of the Nazi take-over of the Prussian police apparatus.

Göring's love of uniforms and of the disguises that uniforms made possible provided cartoonists with an easy target. Göring helped Hitler to eliminate the communists and he also assisted Hitler in the action against Röhm and the SA. One drawing by Bert points out that aspect of Göring's activities (p. 15).

Amongst the top rank of Nazi leaders Heinrich Himmler, the police and security chief, was the most anonymous. Until the war, he had attracted little attention from the artists although there are a few cartoons of him later. Among the minor figures the turnover of personnel over the years was high, and there were few memorable faces and characters in it, perhaps with the exception of Julius Streicher. A former school-teacher, Streicher was a dedicated anti-semitic theorist and publicist. The newspaper he edited, *Der Stürmer,* plumbed lower depths, in the cause of anti-semitism, than did the gutter press. Two drawings link the cause — Streicher and his anti-semitism — and the effect — the pornographic public pillorying of a girl who 'went out with a Jew'.

Custodian of the 'New Order' in Europe, Boris Efimov 1942 (above), and *Budapest*, George Whitelaw (above left) *Heinrich Himmler, the top Nazi policeman and leader of the SS, was the most sinister of the Nazi leaders and the one responsible for the concentration camps and the implementation of Nazi race policies. As Efimov points out, drawing on Himmler's own words, the goal of the SS was to create a 'new order' aimed at organizing Europe economically and politically on a basis that would destroy all pre-existing boundaries. This, of course, meant nothing short of European domination and Efimov aptly presents him as a menacing spider spreading out across the map of Europe. A similar image is used to show Himmler as a monstrous, four-armed beast with staring eyes and the symbol of the skull and crossbones on his cap, his clawing talons sweeping across Budapest and the rest of Hungary.*

Streicher, Bert (left) and *The Result*, Eric Godal (below left) *Julius Streicher, one of Hitler's earliest supporters and a fanatical anti-semite, waged a bitter and relentless campaign against the Jews in his gutter newspaper, Der Stürmer. The paper was a great success and by 1937 was selling about half a million copies. It was an effective vehicle for propaganda, as Godal's caricature shows, depicting the barbaric treatment of a girl who had gone out with a Jew.*

He Must Have Been Mad, David Low, *Evening Standard*, 15 May 1941 (above); *Can't We Be Friends?*, Philip Zec, *Daily Mirror*,
16 May 1941 (opposite above) and *Dead Men Tell No Tales*, Vicky, *News Chronicle*, 14 May 1941 (opposite below)
*As Hitler's formal deputy Rudolf Hess was an important figure in the Reich. On 10 May 1941, shortly after Hitler's attack on the
Soviet Union, he crash-landed in a Messerschmitt-110 fighter in Scotland. Hitler, who was then staying at Berghof, his retreat in the
Alps, was stunned when he heard the news. Rudolf Hess was a student of Professor Haushofer, the pioneer of the science of
'geopolitics' and Hitler blamed Haushofer for Hess's flight to Britain. Hess was not given a chance to deliver his message that
Germany would guarantee Britain her empire in return for a free hand in Europe. Hess and his flight was a difficult theme for
cartoonists to handle: David Low's solution was to take neither Hess nor his self-imposed mission seriously, whereas Vicky's
implication that Hitler considered Hess as expendable as some other Nazi leaders is misleading.*

Hitler — A German Fate, Paul Weber, 1932

The Thousand Year Reich

Hitler's state presented a serious face to the outside world, and to its citizens. Such humour — cartoons, jokes, stories — as appeared in the press was licensed. Goebbels approved of jokes against the Jews, the communists, and even liberals, but, he said, 'a joke ceases to be a joke when it touches on holiest matters of the national state' — Hitler, the Nazi movement, the racial state, and presumably himself. After one of the David Low's anti-Nazi cartoons was printed in the *Evening Standard* in 1933, British newspapers which printed Low's cartoons were banned in Germany (see below, p. 97).

The Nazis tried to develop their own humour, free from all corrupting influences, especially Jewish. The town council of Hambourg, for instance, resolved to support 'sound' National Socialist literature. It established a prize for the best satirical story, which would best reflect the wit and humour of the north German region. The prize money, a generous 1,000 RM, was awarded to one Hanns ut Haum for a story called *Das Magdalenenhaus* which described a visit to a house for fallen girls by a solemn philanthropic society, accompanied by a reporter, whom the girls welcomed with the familiar greeting, *Servus Egon*. However, the story had been plagiarized from one written by the well-known Prague Jewish journalist Egon Erwin Kisch. Kisch made much fun of the Hamburg town council, and the SS organ,

Das Schwarze Korps, severely rebuked the councillors for their credulity.

Das Schwarze Korps described the incident as 'shameless smuggling of typically foreign forms of thought into the sphere of the National Socialist nation and of its morals'. Anti-semitic cartoons in *Der Stürmer* were always abominable, but the *Berliner Lokalanzeiger* hit the depths when the Jewish writer, Ernst Toller, committed suicide in exile and it published a drawing with the title of one of Toller's books *Hoppla, wir leben!* (Hurrah, we live!) to *Hoppla, ihr sterbt! Deutschland aber lebt!* (Hurrah you die! But Germany lives!).

After Hitler came to power criticism of the Nazi regime was either pushed underground, or abroad. Books were publicly burned, certain authors banned and censorship imposed on the press. Inside the Reich, an isolated, absurd mistake was made in December 1934. Ernst Hanfstaengl's *Tat gegen Tinte* (Action against Ink) was a book of cartoons of Hitler and its blurb stated that it had been seen and expressly approved by the Führer himself. However, the author unwittingly included certain cartoons critical of Hitler and the Nazis and the book did not quite serve its intended purpose of proving how brave Hitler was to fight words with deeds. By then, mass media in Germany had been made uniformly dull in support of the Nazi regime.

In 1934 Prague became the centre of anti-Nazi exiles from Germany. Czechoslovakia was then in

ADOLF – DER ÜBERMENSCH

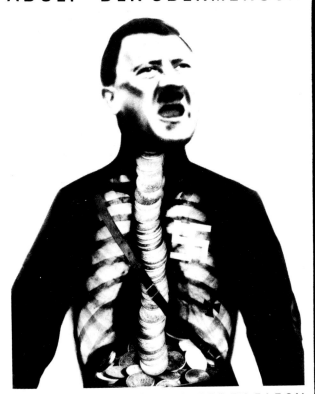

SCHLUCKT GOLD UND REDET BLECH

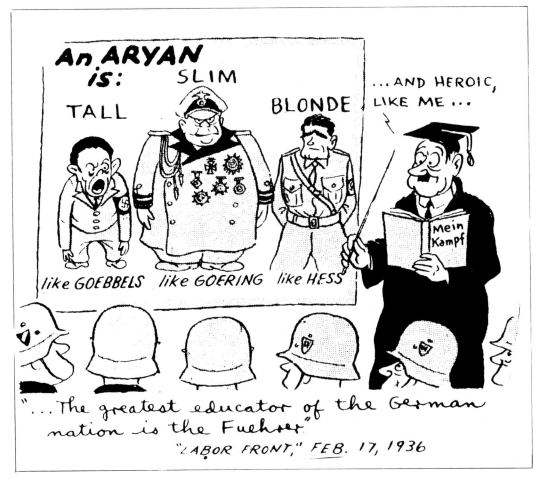

Adolf, the Superman! Swallows Gold and Talks Crap, John Heartfield, 17 July 1932 (far left); A Pure-Blooded Aryan, H. Dobrzyński (centre left); Yes Sir! We're All Aryans, Vaughn Shoemaker, Chicago Daily News, 1938 (left); An Aryan is . . . , 1936 (below far left); The Blood Test, Eric Godal (below centre); For the Increase of the German Race, Eric Godal (below right).

Germany's leaders did not quite come up to the highest Nazi specifications for pure race, nor, like Mussolini, did all their allies. The Nazi tough (below centre) says to the dejected girl whose bed he has just left, 'Marry you? Out of the question. You are just an Eastern-Slavonic type.' In contrast, Godal's fat German is only too eager to follow Hitler's directive to increase the Nordic races.

It Worked at the Reichstag — Why Not Here?, David Low, *Evening Standard*, 18 October 1933
Low's cartoon comments on one of Hitler's first calculated gambles in foreign affairs. On 14 October 1933 he announced that Germany was withdrawing from the League of Nations because she had not been given equality of treatment with all other nations at Geneva, especially in armaments. Low depicts a triumphant Hitler setting fire to the League's headquarters while Mussolini, Daladier (the French premier) and Sir John Simon (Britain's foreign minister) look on from an upstairs window. The means of putting out the fire — economic sanctions — remains untouched.

Hitler   Mussolini   Daladier Simon

IT WORKED AT THE REICHSTAG—WHY NOT HERE ?

the concluding stages of Thomas Masaryk's presidency, being the only one of the small states of Central and Eastern Europe which had emerged from the ruins of the Habsburg monarchy and which was still a working democracy. It also had a culturally active, German-speaking, partly Jewish minority and a left-wing, Czech and mainly communist community of writers and artists. The *Prager Tagblatt* was one of the leading Central European dailies, and there was a good German theatre in Prague, as well as a German university. Thomas and Heinrich Mann, John Heartfield, Wieland Herzfelde and other German intellectuals came to Czechoslovakia after Hitler's take-over of power in Berlin.

Newspapers and publishing houses moved to Prague as well. Heartfield, together with the writers Hermann Leopold and Fritz Ergenbeck, were on the editorial staff of the exiled *AIZ* and Franz Carl Weiskopf was its editor-in-chief. It published a photomontage by Heartfield almost every week (previously, during the Weimar period, the newspaper was a monthly), despite the adverse conditions of exile and difficult access to new photographic material. But *AIZ* in Prague catered for a small readership and by 1936 its circulation had dropped to 12,000 copies. The editors tried to smuggle pocket editions of the newspaper into Germany, as well as postcards of Heartfield's work, but without much success. Some of the

postcards were sent to Julius Streicher, so that he would not complain that people were working behind his back. By 1938, however, the introduction of preventive censorship in Czechoslovakia began severely to affect the contents of *AIZ* and, soon, Heartfield and his friends started leaving Central Europe for the safer shores of Britain and America.

The *Malik Verlag* also moved from Berlin to Prague with Wieland Herzfelde and started making available to German readers works by anti-fascist authors: Konrad Heiden's *Geburt des dritten Reiches* (The Birth of the Third Reich), Ignazio Silone's *Der Faschismus*, Walther Rode's *Deutschland ist Caliban*, C. and V. Michaelis' and W. O. Somin's *Die Braune Kultur*. There were several weeklies then published in German in Prague which belonged to the anti-fascist camp — *Die Wahrheit* (Truth), *Aufruf* (Proclamation), *Die neue Weltbühne* (The New World Scene) — as well as a satirical weekly, *Simplicus*. It was the Simplicus Verlag which published, in Prague as early as 1934, a collection of cartoons called *Das Dritte Reich in der Karikatur* (The Third Reich in Caricature). In the introduction Heinrich Mann described Hitler's Reich as the German Spiesser's (a rude word for petty bourgeois) 'horn of plenty', a world created for the *Turner* and *Säufer*, the nationalist gymnasts and drunks, and for people such as the right-wing anti-semitic Professors

The Third Reich in Caricature, (left)
The cover of the volume of cartoons which resulted from the exhibition in Prague in April–May 1934.

Rühs and Fries, who had forced Heinrich Heine out of Germany. Mann pointed out the two striking features of the Third Reich: the combination of energy and cowardice, and added that its masters 'do not know the world. Their own lives were spent between jails, mental hospitals and night clubs.'

The collection of cartoons was the by-product of an exhibition at the Mánes Arts Club in April–May 1934, which caused a diplomatic incident. John Heartfield was represented by thirty-six photomontages at the exhibition, and the Germans found the picture *Adolf, the Superman, Swallows Gold and Talks Crap* especially offensive. Two German diplomatic protests were followed by similar Austrian, Italian and Polish representations to the Czechoslovak government. The controversy attracted many visitors to the exhibition, and much favourable comment on the work of the anti-fascist artists in the press. From Paris, Henri Barbusse and Paul Signac expressed their solidarity with the artists who showed their work in Prague.

The idea of government officials — first the German Minister to Prague, Dr Koch, who was later joined by the Austrian, the Italian and Polish Ministers — expressing the views of their governments on matters concerning art, was ironic in itself, and was seen as such by the local press. For the first time, Hitler's regime made an attempt to extend cultural and media *Gleichschaltung* (uniformity) outside the frontiers of Germany. The

Czech painter, Karel Teige, commented in the newspaper *Doba* on 24 May 1934: 'The exhibition of cartoons and satirical drawings had become in the present circumstances an extraordinarily important artistic anti-fascist manifestation, an occasion for a confrontation between fascist reaction and the anti-fascist left on the cultural front.'

The collection, *Das Dritte Reich in der Karikatur*, which appeared soon after the Mánes exhibition, was of a high artistic standard, giving an accurate and detailed reflection of the face of the Third Reich. The brutality of the SA, the character of the Nazi leaders, of Hitler in particular, and of the Nazi

JOSEF ČAPEK, brother of Karel, the writer and dramatist, was born in 1887. Čapek spent some years working for *Lidové Noviny*, the leading Prague quality daily. He was also co-author with his brother Karel of two plays. Like most of the Czech cartoonists of his generation, Čapek rejected the elaborate detail of the French school of caricature and instead adopted the sophisticated simplicity of the *Simplicissimus* artists. Čapek spent the war in a concentration camp and died in a hunger march in 1945.

The Salon of the Dependents Has Achieved a Great Success, Elkins, *Le Rire*, 3 March 1934 (right)
The drawing commemorates Hitler's laying of the foundation stone for the House of German Art in Munich in 1934.

Art Has Become Very Spontaneous and Sincere Under the Supervision of National Socialism, Stephen Roth (below)
Roth's text is taken from Goebbels. In reality those artists who failed to produce Nazi-approved art were visited by 'aesthetic officials' who had at their disposal a wide range of sanctions, including force.

Memorial to the 'Sculptors of Germany', Oskar Garvens, *Kladderadatsch*, 1933 (opposite)
Garvens' caricature works on two levels. It compares 'decadent' sculpture with the pseudo-classical muscular nudes favoured by Hitler but also makes a point about the 'sculptors' or architects of the German state since World War I. The liberal, faction-torn republic of which the Jews were an integral part is smashed by Hitler who in its place creates the 'German Hercules', symbol of the Nazi culture.

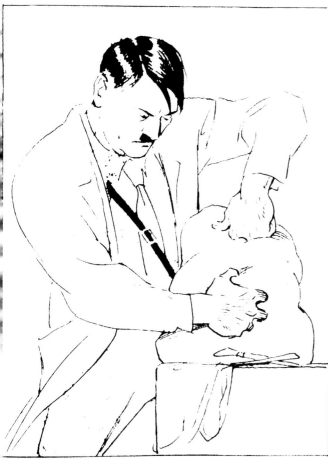
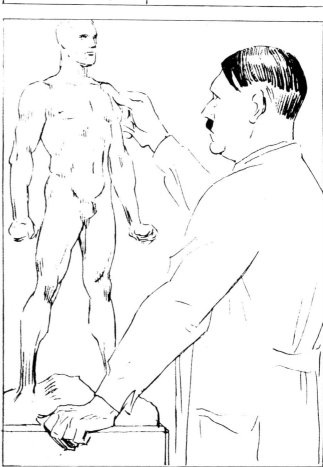

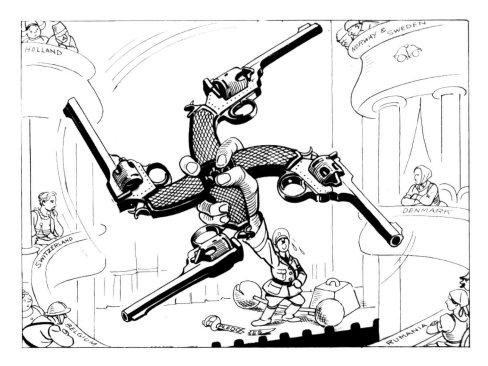

Can He Keep it Up?, Daily Express, 22 January 1940 (left) and *Whither Cock?* (right), Bert Strube 1941
Once Germany had been conquered within, Hitler lost no time in turning to foreign policy. But where he would strike next was a matter of some conjecture, as these caricatures show.

Starting the Fireworks, Vaughn Shoemaker, *Chicago Daily News,* 26 April 1933 (far right)
Shoemaker's cartoon suggests that in taking over the powers of the various state governments — a process begun after the 1933 Reichstag fire and completed in 1934 — the Nazis were stirring up more opposition than they could handle. However, the artist underestimated Hitler and his capacity to turn a potential disaster to his advantage.

movement, and Hitler's racial policies were all well covered in the book. Hitler's obsession with purity of race and with the value of Aryan blood was reflected in a comprehensive body of laws. The first of these appeared in the spring of 1933, and they aimed at stopping racial decadence with the renewal of the German nation by the 'deliberate breeding of a new man'. There were a number of drawings on show on the complementary drive for racial purity. The idiotic fussiness of the National Socialists about race was brutally summed up by Godal in his drawing *The Blood Test.*

One of the major contributors to *Das Dritte Reich in der Karikatur* was Josef Čapek. His drawings were simple, pure and hard-hitting; and they were ideally suited for newspapers. His early work concentrated on the elaborate mockery of social types before he moved on to sharp satire of Czech political life. From the time of Hitler's rise to power, Čapek, as well as other Prague artists, began to look more closely at the rest of Europe and in particular at the spread of fascism. The imagery is particularly powerful in Čapek's drawing 'Now let the degenerate democracies show . . .' from his series, *A Dictator's Boots.*

Hitler's insistence on the value of non-decadent art was combined with his self-importance in Adolf Hoffmeister's drawing (p. 87); the same point was made, in a visually more complicated way, and probably earlier, by Elkins in the French satirical

weekly *Le Rire* (Laughter), on 3 March 1934. The drawing (p. 72) referred to the laying of the foundation stone for the House of Art in Munich, when Hitler declared that 'It is marvellous to live in a time which sets people great tasks.' The title of the cartoon was *The Salon of the Dependents Has Achieved a Great Success.* The point about Hitler's view of art was probably made most successfully by Garvens. He showed the Führer smashing a 'decedent' sculpture and then making the kind of sculpture he thought fit for the Germans to admire. Apart from summing up Hitler's aesthetic theory, Garvens effectively portrayed Hitler's characteristic gestures in the four drawings (p. 73).

National Socialist attitudes to religion and the churches were also the butt of satirical comment. Godal hinted that Christ's Jewish grandmother might be held against him (p. 76). After January 1933 Hitler attempted to bring all the Protestant Churches together under Nazi patronage. One cartoon showed that this was not without its difficulties.

More effectively, Hitler's regime made the legal and the academic professions serve its own ends. Although the Reichstag fire trial did not quite go as the regime would have wished, and the Bulgarian communist leader, Dimitrov, scored a notable success during the trial, the judges soon fell into line. Heartfield commented (p. 78) that 'They twist

and turn, and call themselves German judges.'
Those university teachers who remained in
Germany — the vast majority — proved
themselves even more malleable. Lack of civil
courage among the academics was pointed to in
Kladderadatsch early in 1933: 'What do you think
about the take-over of government by the national
cabinet?' 'I am sorry, but I have no view, I deal only
with the second half of the fifteenth
century' (p. 79).

The people who observed Hitler carefully at a
close range had difficulty working out his motives
and intentions. This happened in connection with
his foreign policy after 1933. A number of later
cartoons were to pick the right targets for Hitler's
aggression; but as late as 1941 there was no
certainty about the order in which they would be
attacked. In the drawing which appeared on
15 March 1933, in the satirical Alsace journal
Franc-Tireur (Sharpshooter), the poor, ill-used
German Michael was expected eagerly to follow
his leader as he had done before in history. Urging
him on are shadowy, imperious, historical figures.
Hitler's ambiguity in matters of war and peace was
shown in *The Nation* published in New York in 1933
(see pages 80–81). Out of Hitler's mouth,
attached to the end of a cannon, flies the dove of
peace (see page 80). The drawing is similar to one
of Heartfield's montages, which appeared on
7 June 1933 (p. 80) entitled *He Will Gas the World*

with His Phrases, with the text: 'The man who
swore on the German constitution speaks now of
peace. He will keep it as he kept his oath.' The
dove of peace occurs again in a Yugoslav cartoon
published in October 1933 and entitled *Pacifist
Hitler* (p. 81).

By the end of 1934 a considerable amount of
critical information existed on the Nazi regime as
well as the character of its leaders. Such
information had, however, two limitations. First of
all, it was largely confined to Central Europe;
secondly, it was most often propagated by men
and women who broadly belonged to the socialist
and communist movements. Adolf Hitler, in a
country which was susceptible to the threat from
the east, made political capital out of his fight
against *Bolschewismus*. By exploiting the
middle- and lower-middle class unease which
derived from Lenin's revolution in Russia and its
consequences, he made his regime acceptable to
those Germans and others whose fears of a
socialist revolution were stronger than their
compassion or political sense. But whatever the
political persuasions of the artists shown here,
they attacked the Nazi regime with wit, and often
with prophetic insight.

They even anticipated the attitudes of some
historians of the period, expressed many years
later. One such view was of Hitler as an unnatural,
inhuman creature with a diabolical nature without

Can You Prove You Had an Aryan Grandmother?, Eric Godal, 1934 (right)
Godal's caricature, suggesting that Christ would have had difficulties with Nazi racial policies, picks on the Nazi Party's leanings towards a nebulous Teutonic paganism and on the German churches' ambivalent attitude to the Jewish question; neither the Catholic nor Protestant churches took a firm or consistent stand on the persecution of the Jews.

German Churches' Truce, Eric Godal, 1934 (below) *The Nazification of the German Protestant churches was hampered, at first, by divisions within the Church due largely to its regional divergencies. Although the Reich Church was finally established in July 1933, there was sharp disagreement among the various church organizations over who should be the first Reich bishop. An end was soon put to that by suspending several church dignitaries and leaving the SA and the Gestapo to deal with the rest. Hitler's candidate, Ludwig Müller, became Reich bishop.*

The New Christiantity, See? 100 % Aryan, Philip Zec, *Daily Mirror*, 16 January 1941 (far right)
Some of the leading Nazis aimed to replace Christianity with the paganism of the early Germanic gods.

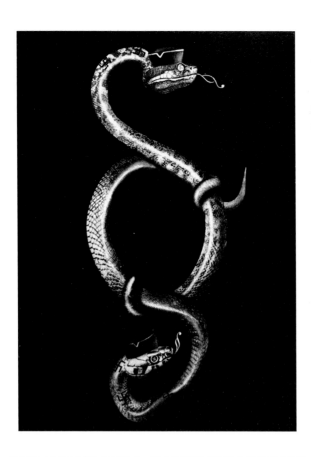

They Twist and Turn and Call Themselves German Judges, John Heartfield, 10 October 1933 (left)
Heartfield's two entwined adders wearing judges' caps form a symbol used in German legal documents. While the majority of the legal profession may not have held Nazi beliefs, they were authoritarian by tradition, and were soon brought into line after 1933.

Hitler Has No Use for Intellectuals Like Einstein, Seppla (Josef Plank), *Die Brennessel, c.* 1933 (right)
Before 1933 Jews had accounted for 12 per cent of all German professors and a quarter of her Nobel Prize winners, of whom Einstein was one. Swept out by the 'Nazi broom' in 1933, he emigrated to the USA. Other scientists also left the country, thus depriving Germany of the world leadership in natural sciences she had hitherto enjoyed — and was never to recover. Einstein is shown being 'swept' from his Potsdam laboratory, the 'Einsteinturm.'

German Academics, Dollinger, *Kladderadatsch*, 1933 (far right)
One remarkable feature of Hitler's early months in power was the speed with which the academic and legal professions fell into line. This caricature pinpoints the indifference to the overthrow of democracy expressed by many academics. The text reads: 'What do you think about the take-over of government by the national cabinet?' Reply: 'I'm sorry, but I have no view, I deal only with the second half of the fifteenth century.'

JOHN HEARTFIELD was born Helmut Herzfelde in Berlin in 1891, the son of a socialist poet who wrote under the name of Franz Held. By 1913 he was working as a printer's designer, producing book jackets and advertising work. After the outbreak of World War I he began writing pacifist poetry and changed his name although the authorities refused to register it. Instead of going to the front with his regiment in 1915 he was committed to a hospital for nervous disorders. He was released after a few months and became a rather negligent postman in the Grünewald district of Berlin. In 1917 he founded the Malik Verlag with his brother Wieland, and became a film director in the UFA company. In the following year he became a member of the Berlin Club Dada and joined the newly founded German Communist Party. In the following years he designed Dadaist collages with Grosz and various puppet shows and programmes for Max Reinhardt's cabaret; and from 1920 to 1922 he designed the scenery and costumes for several plays produced by Reinhardt. After fleeing to Prague in 1933 and then to England in 1938 he returned to East Berlin after the war and died there in 1968.

precedent. This view was reflected in several cartoons; and it was put forward by Karl Radek, the leading Soviet politician and propagandist, when commenting on the outcome of the 1930 elections in Germany: 'Nothing like this has happened in the history of political struggle, especially in a country with well-established political differences, in which every new party has had to fight for every position held by the established parties. Nothing is more characteristic than the fact that nothing has been said about this party either in bourgeois or in socialist literature, a party which has now assumed the second place in German political life. It is a party without history which suddenly emerges into German political life, just as an island suddenly emerges in the middle of the sea because of volcanic activity.'[1]

More often, the Nazi movement was described not as an island which suddenly floated up in the sea, but as a movement for which the German past had prepared the way. The links with German myths were strongly established by the most perceptive artists; with myths both ancient and modern and, especially, with ancient myths in their nineteenth-century German garb. The cosmic tragedies of the *Nibelungen Ring*, the twin desire for a pure past and a pure race, all the *Blut und Boden* — blood and soil — cant, were paraded not only for their ridiculous values but because they really did provide the Nazis with much of their

intellectual baggage.[2] Many critics ascribed a specifically German quality to Nazism — a view accepted, much later, by French- and English-speaking historians. Pedigrees were constructed linking Hitler and Bismarck, Frederick the Great and beyond. William Shirer's (1960) *Rise and Fall of the Third Reich,* for instance, saw fascism as a German phenomenon *par excellence.*

A different view had been expressed in Wilhelm Reich's *Die Massenpsychologie des Faschismus,* first published in 1933, with a second edition appearing in Denmark at the time of the Mánes exhibition in Prague the following year. Reich, a psychiatrist, who had worked on his study in the years 1930–1933, advanced the argument that fascism was a general clinical condition which could affect mankind anywhere. He wrote, 'The structure of fascism is characterized by metaphysical thinking, unorthodox faith, obsession with abstract ethical ideals, and belief in the divine predestination of the *Führer*.'[3] The Marxists, Reich argued, underrated the political value of myth in their analysis and political practice, and he regarded their socio-economic explanation of fascism as inadequate. He belived that fascism was not an ideology or action of any single ethnic or political group, but was an expression of the irrational character structure of the average human being, whose primary biological needs and impulses had been suppressed over thousands of

years. Reich hinted at the social function of such suppression, and the key role in the process played by the family and the church. He insisted that every form of organized mysticism — of which the Nazi movement was an example — was based on the unsatisfied needs of the masses. Be that as it may, the artists who exhibited their work at the Mánes show in Prague in the spring of 1934, many of whom were German, would have found Reich's argument rather than Shirer's more acceptable. They knew well that there existed another Germany; they themselves were part of it.

The Nation, New York.

The Dove, Georges, *The Nation*, 1933 (above, far left); *German
Michael Ready to Do Battle*, *Franc-Tireur*, 15 March 1933 (left);
He Will Gas the World with His Phrases, John Heartfield, 7 June
1933 (below far left) and *Pacifist Hitler*, *Jutro*, 19 October 1933
(above)
*Hitler talked of peace but prepared for war. Neither in New York
nor in Ljubljana did Hitler's peace-loving phrases sound
credible: Heartfield whose photomontage appeared soon after
Hitler's 'peace speech' (17 May 1933) bitterly and correctly
predicts: 'The man who swore on the German constitution
speaks now of peace. He will keep it as he kept his oath.' The
hollowness of those peace proposals was reinforced in
October when Hitler announced Germany's withdrawal from the
League of Nations.*

This is the House That Diplomacy Built, David Fitzpatrick, *St Louis Post-Dispatch*, 7 April 1935

Matters of War and Peace

Soon after Hitler came to power in January 1933 the centre of satirical attack on the Nazi regime moved away from Germany. Indeed, between 1933 and 1938, a broadly based international campaign against Hitler and his government was reflected in, and assisted by, caricature. In the course of its development abroad, the nature and style of cartooning against Hitler underwent a change. In the early stages of his career when he received only occasional attention, the artists, especially George Grosz, Karl Arnold and Paul Weber, were concerned in their work with the personality of Hitler and the nature of the Nazi movement. In the early 1930s these early statements were amplified and extended, as the exhibition in Prague in May 1934 showed. The Nazis' racial attitudes and policies, their leaders' intellectual pretensions, Hitler's faithlessness towards his friends and associates were all incisively depicted.

But the dispersal of the artists, the broadening of the campaign against Hitler and the increasing pace of Germany's initiatives abroad partly wiped out the subtleties of the earlier portraits. The artists who left Germany lost the political and social hinterland which had nourished them, as well as the easy access to the German media. Now the missiles aimed at Hitler's movement had to cross frontiers; their construction therefore was different. They illustrated, in some, often reliable, detail, the progress of Hitler's

international ambition; less often were they able to address themselves to the effect of Hitler's rule on Germany itself.

In Britain, political dividing lines on the growth of totalitarian movements on the Continent were drawn early — well before Hitler came to power. Mussolini's stern dealings with socialist and liberal opponents, for example, encouraged the foundation of the British Fascist Party which was supported by Lord Rothermere's *Daily Mail*, the largest mass circulation daily. The New Zealand born caricaturist David Low added Rothermere to his gallery of characters, 'in a black shirt helping to stoke the fires of class hatred'. Low's attitudes to Mussolini and to Hitler and their translation into his drawings, provide a sharp insight into caricature in the years before and during the war. They also reveal the extent and limitations of artists' political influence.

Many caricaturists, like photographers, use their art to illustrate and comment on the movement of politics, rather than to influence them. Yet it can be argued that great caricaturists like George Grosz or Paul Weber helped to shape public attitudes towards Hitler's movement, even if those attitudes, and the political position they represented, suffered a defeat in Germany in 1933. David Low also belonged to the small group of artists who not only illustrated but also influenced public events.

Low was doubly fortunate. He could resist

Ethiopia Menaces Italy, Josef Novak, 1935 (left)
Mussolini invaded Ethiopia on 3 October 1935 in defiance of the Covenant of the League of Nations. Just how threatening the poor inhabitants of this ancient kingdom were is shown in this Czech cartoon.

The Krupp Baby Bottle, J. Sennep (right)
Although he is a mere baby in the arms race, Hitler is growing strong and healthy as he feeds on the products of the Krupp armaments factory. To western democratic politicians, who scamper away, he says: 'Your good health, my little fathers!'

Hurrah, the Butter is Gone! John Heartfield, 19 December 1935 (far right)
Hartfield's sinister photomontage on German rearmament carries a quote from Göring: Empires have always grown strong on iron ore; butter and lard have, at best, made a nation fat!'

manipulation by politicians, and he aimed his darts at Hitler from a politically powerful base. He was possessed with the quality of courage, even in other, more local contexts. For instance, he attacked British imperialism at a time when it was not fashionable to do so.[1] (In contrast, Paul Weber allowed himself to be manipulated by Goebbels and his illustrations of British Imperialism to be used for propaganda purposes.) But even when Low addressed himself to a foreign subject, he sometimes had to resist pressure at home.

The combination of Low's talent and inventiveness and the accidental fact that he worked for a free British press raised him high above the ranks of ordinary newspaper

ADOLF HOFFMEISTER was born in Prague in 1902. While studying law he began writing articles which he often illustrated with his own drawings. He visited Italy, France and England and in 1931 the USSR. He regularly worked as a political cartoonist, and like Pelc violently attacked Hitler and his movement. He left Prague in 1938 and eventually settled in the USA. He wrote a humorous account of his departure from Prague and his subsequent adventures before arriving in America in *The Animals are in Cages.*

cartoonists. But in America, the Soviet Union, France and in other parts of the world, there were other accomplished craftsmen who charted the progress of international politics with its brutality and corruption. As the war approached, the campaign against Hitler gained in intensity. The American press in particular reflected that process. With its richness and variety of local newspapers, its many ethnic minorities whose members had not cut entirely loose from their countries of origin, and its often first-rate foreign reporting, America was in a good position to follow and assess the progress of Hitler's ambition.

The international order which had been imposed after World War I contained the seeds of its own destruction. It disregarded the principles on which it was allegedly constructed; it sharply divided Europe into states which benefited from the war and those which suffered from their defeat; it created artificial boundaries and corridors. It rested on enforcement rather than consensus, and could survive only as long as the wartime alliance of America, Britain and France remained united and preserved its influence in Europe. It was clear, early in 1935, that the order had little future: David Fitzpatrick made this point strongly in a cartoon in the *St Louis Post-Dispatch* entitled *This is the House That Diplomacy Built* (p. 82).

Hitler tried to exploit the flaws and contradictions in the peace treaties so that his

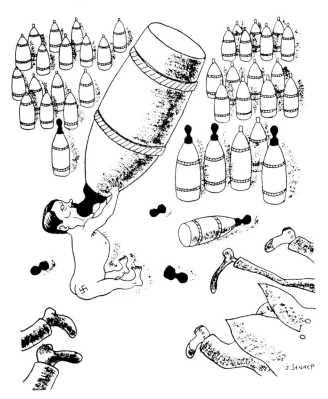

Hurrah, die Butter ist alle!

Goering in seiner Hamburger Rede: „Erz hat stets ein Reich stark gemacht, Butter und Schmalz haben höchstens ein Volk fett gemacht"

foreign policy threatened almost every state in Europe. Although he declared in a speech made in January 1941 'No human being had declared or recorded what he wanted more often than I. Again and again I wrote these words: "The abolition of the Treaty of Versailles!"'[2], nevertheless to observers in the mid-1930s Hitler's intentions appeared less clear-cut. There was no singleness of purpose in his foreign policy; he used ambiguity as a weapon abroad as much as he did at home. He did not present himself only as an opponent of the peace settlements, nor as a defender of German interests in Europe. Fears of revolutionary threat from the East had not disappeared, and middle-class western Europe was largely anti-communist. Hitler therefore used his anti-Bolshevik trump card with deliberation. He assumed easily, and just as easily discarded, the role of leader of an alternative form of government, which could replace representative democracy; he exploited anti-semitism where it already existed. Images of Hitler as a foreign-policy maker dissolved into each other as he swiftly moved from one opportunity to another.

The large German minorities in Czechoslovakia and in Poland, as well as in the German state of Austria, Hitler's birthplace, were at first hardly seen by him as an object of foreign policy; instead they were an internal German matter. In July 1934 a premature Nazi coup in Vienna resulted in the murder of the Austrian Chancellor, Dollfuss; the *putsch* failed and from then on, Hitler used Nazi Germans abroad more carefully and in much less of a hurry. A few months later he achieved a spectacular success in the Saarland plebiscite in January 1935 when some 2,000 votes were cast for a union with France against 445,000 for reunion with Germany and 46,000 for the continuation of the status quo — that is, administration of the province by the League of Nations. A few months later, on 18 June, the Anglo-German Naval Pact was signed. It was the 120th anniversary of Waterloo, where the British and the Prussians had defeated the French. By accepting Germany as a partner in negotiations concerning armaments, the pact marked the end of the Versailles era. International relationships were shaken as a result of the Anglo-German naval agreements, and rearranged.

Despite ideological affinities with Hitler's regime, Mussolini had been more apprehensive of the German menace than most European politicians. Austria stood between Hitler and him and the abortive Nazi *putsch* in Austria prompted mutual suspicion as portrayed by Eric Godal in a cartoon *The Chess Match Begins* (p. 91). But soon Mussolini came closer to Hitler and pursued reckless foreign policies. The Italian adventure in Ethiopia established a new low in the conduct of warfare by an industrial European state on a

85

Dreaming France, Paul Iribe, *Le Témoin*, 1933
Iribe satirizes the western democracies' acceptance of Hitler's protestations of peace and non-aggression. France dreams sweet dreams, oblivious of the economic troubles and political upheavals beyond the border.

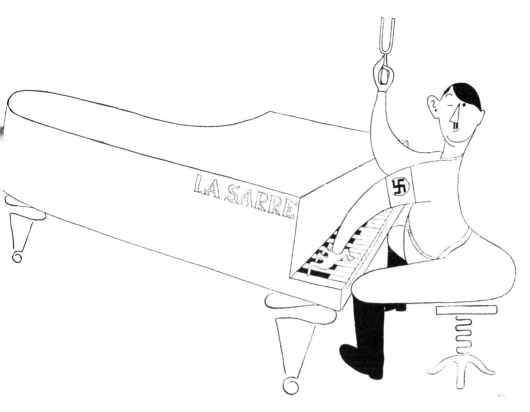

The Saar Question, Adolf Hoffmeister, 1935 (left) and *Saar Plebiscite*, Bert Strube, *Daily Express*, London, 16 January 1935 (below)
The Saar plebiscite of January 1935 was the first triumph of Nazi propaganda abroad. When the coal-rich territory voted overwhelmingly to return to the Reich, Hitler publicly declared that he had no further claims on France, a remark which Hoffmeister, if not the diplomats, took with scepticism. Seated at a piano and holding a tuning fork Hitler declares: 'I have created harmony in the Saar, now for Alsace-Lorraine.' Strube depicts the Saar inhabitants as a flock of sheep going blindly into the Nazi 'pen.' Although communists and Jews are separated out, the rest are branded with the Nazi stamp.

Hitler
ANVIL WEDDINGS ARE MORE ROMANTIC

virtually defenceless enemy, its nature being shown in the drawing *Ethiopia Menaces Italy* (p. 84). In May 1936 Mussolini declared that the Roman Empire had again appeared on the 'fated hills of Rome'.

Hitler preached peace but continued to arm; in response to his policies John Heartfield used a sentence from a speech by Göring: 'Empires have always grown strong on iron ore; butter and lard have at best made a nation fat', as a text for his photomontage *Hurrah, the Butter is Gone!* (p. 85). Hitler's portrait has been hung in place of Hindenburg's, ironically close to the framed qutotation from the patriotic poem *Die Wacht am Rhein:* 'Thou canst rest in peace, dear Fatherland!' The Soviet Communist Party organ, *Pravda*, linked Hitler's policy of revenge with the Kaiser's earlier sabre-rattling in an outspoken drawing, on 24 March 1935, entitled *Revenge — Following the Kaiser*. In a way reminiscent of the decades before World War I, a diplomatic possibility emerged in the course of 1935 that Germany would again have to face an East-West alliance. The French began to negotiate a treaty of mutual assistance with the Soviet Union and David Low hinted at the possibility of Germany's isolation in an *Evening Standard* cartoon (p. 91).

But the Soviet-French pact, followed by a similar understanding between Russia and Czechoslovakia, were straws in the wind. There was the solid achievement, on Hitler's part, of the naval agreement with Britain and the increasingly evident desire, on Britain's part, to appease the increasingly menacing dictator. Hitler exploited the period before the ratification of the Franco-Soviet treaty by moving the German army into the demilitarized Rhineland in March 1936. His assessment of the French capacity to resist the move was low, and events proved him right. He followed up the breach of two international treaties with an offer of alliance to France, a promise to return to the League of Nations — he had taken Germany out of the international organization in 1933 — and of general good behaviour by Germany. By then, the way Hitler treated the 'spineless leaders of democracy' — with utter contempt — could hardly be overlooked.

On 25 July 1936 Hitler took the decision to support General Franco against the constitutional government of Spain. Antonin Pelc portrayed Franco's dance of death in *Señorita Franco* (p. 93). Picasso's famous painting, *Guernica*, underscored the theme of utter defencelessness of the civilian population against the modern war machine — a tragic theme which was soon repeated in other parts of Europe. Otherwise, the suffering of the Spanish population, as well as the local political conflicts which contributed to it, did not lend themselves easily to satirical treatment; only the external forces, which became locked in conflict on

Der Zweck vons Janze
„Olympiagäste, im Gleichschritt — marsch!"

Anvil Weddings are More Romantic, David Low, *Evening Standard*, 25 January 1937 (far left)
Low's cartoon on the 'guns before butter' theme shows Hitler wedded to a policy of belt-tightening with military intent, ignoring the call for international co-operation.

Goebbels' Puppets, John Heartfield, 1 July 1936 (left)
The Olympic Games, held in Berlin in 1936, gave Goebbels a golden opportunity to show off to the world the achievements of the Third Reich. The caption below reads, in Berlin dialect: 'The object of the exercise — All together, Olympic visitors — quick march!'

Spanish soil, were visible more clearly. With a certain transatlantic detachment Fitzpatrick (p. 90) contrasted the Spanish conflagration in its opening stages with the ghoulish interest and mutual distrust of the other European powers. In Spain, World War II was rehearsed in earnest; the commitment of the western European Left, with the participation of the Soviet Union, inevitably brought together the two European fascist powers in the Berlin-Rome Axis. In the *St Louis Post-Dispatch* Fitzpatrick portrayed the Napoleonic ambitions of Hitler and of Mussolini, and in Spain they were playing for larger stakes than they had done hitherto.

The German reoccupation of the demilitarized Rhineland in 1936 was an act of defiance with far-reaching implications, but the Olympic games in Berlin in the same year went far to pacify and test international opinion. The plan to hold them had been made before Hitler came to power, but it was the Nazi regime which hugely benefited from them. A Potemkin village operation was launched in the capital; house owners were ordered to keep their front gardens in impeccable order; traces of anti-Nazi slogans were wiped out; even anti-semitic propaganda was temporarily suspended. When Hitler opened the games on 1 August, the French team honoured him with the Nazi salute. Hitler's regime succeeded, for the first time in the history of sport, in politicizing a sporting event: a theme which was thoroughly worked on by John Heartfield. The way Goebbels exploited the Olympic athletes was elegantly summarized in the photomontage which made clever use of the Olympic emblem.

Towards the end of 1937 Hitler was growing restless. He was concerned that the process which he had set in motion in Germany might lose its momentum and that the 'leap to the great final goals' might be missed. It was during this time that the gearing of German society and economy for an all-out effort was set into motion. As early as autumn 1936 Hitler indicated that the country's industrial production would have to be speeded up to provide the basis for a policy of expansion. Göring was put in charge of a four-year plan on the Soviet pattern which aimed to make Germany self-sufficient and well armed, without regard to the economic consequences of such policy. Göring told German businessmen and industrialists that economic criteria of production were no longer decisive. In November 1937 the Ministry of Propaganda issued a directive to the press to keep quiet about the preparations for 'total war' which were being carried out in the various branches of the Nazi party. The powers of Heinrich Himmler and of the SS had been greatly increased, the number of concentration camps (first set up in Germany in 1933) had grown, and contingency plans were made for Hitler Youth to

Spectators at the Ringside, David Fitzpatrick, *St Louis Post-Dispatch*, 9 August 1936 (right) and *Non-Intervention Poker*, David Low, *Evening Standard*, 13 January 1937 (below)

The civil war in Spain provided the artists with several themes. There was the complex issue of diplomatic relations surrounding the war and Low and Fitzpatrick did their best to deal with it; the human issue — the utter defencelessness of civilian population against the machinery of war — was dealt with by the cartoonists and, most memorably, by Picasso.

TRUSTFUL TONY:
"JUST TO DISCOURAGE CHEATING, I'LL WEAR A STRAIT-JACKET AND LET YOU BOYS PLAY MY HAND FOR ME "

NON-INTERVENTION POKER

The Chess-Game Begins,
Eric Godal, 1934 (left)
*Godal depicts the mutual
distrust of the two fascist
dictators in the summer of 1934
following the failed Nazi putsch
in Austria; only a month before,
Hitler had promised Mussolini
that he would keep his hands
off Austria. Tension increased
when Mussolini hastily
mobilized four armed battalions
on the Brenner Pass.*

Cause and Effect, David Low,
Evening Standard, May 1935
(below)
*A response to the hastily
signed Franco-Russian Pact
and the Russo-Czechoslovak
Pact, this caricature depicts the
closing of ranks against
Germany. In fact, Hitler
subsequently managed to turn
events to his advantage.*

"See! Who will now deny that I have restored Germany to her former influence in European affairs!"

CAUSE AND EFFECT.

take over as a labour force in the factories.

Hitler even appeared self-confident enough for a confrontation with the Christian churches, an issue he had vacillated over for a long time. The Catholics had been at a tactical disadvantage for some time, despite the declaration of the bishops, in 1936, that the church was ready to help the state with its struggle against Bolshevism. In 1937 several trials took place of members of monastic orders on charges of sexual malpractices, and the regime undermined the position of the Catholic schools by requiring all teachers to swear loyalty and obedience to Hitler. In June the Protestant church was deprived of the control of its finances, and the Protestant opposition was intimidated by a large number of arrests, including the arrest of Pastor Niemöller, one of the leaders of the opposition to the attempts at Nazification of the evangelical churches.

In November 1938 Hitler told German newspaper editors that he had been 'forced by circumstances to talk of peace, almost exclusively, for decades':

It was possible for me to win the German people their freedom gradually, and give them the arms which were always necessary as the prerequisite for the next step, only by constantly stressing Germany's desire for peace and peaceful intentions. It is clear that such peace propaganda, carried on for decades, has its doubtful aspects; it can easily lead to giving many people the idea that the regime is identical with the decision and the desire to preserve peace in all circumstances.[3]

Hitler's diplomatic manoeuvres, made necessary by the exigencies of international relations, or by the exigencies of international relations, or by his policies at home, are only intelligible in the context of his own personal fixations. He was obsessed with the concepts of *Lebensraum*, living space, and of the purity of German — or, in Nazi terminology, Aryan — blood. Both were old and deep obsessions for him, and help to explain Hitler's immense drive, and his ultimate failure. The myth of *Blut und Boden* provided the moving and unifying force, underpinning Hitler's policies at home and abroad.

Whenever he contemplated the future, Hitler was far from comforted. At dinner in his headquarters during the war he told his audience that he was glad the technological age was only in its infancy during his lifetime. Hitler seems to have found radical change difficult to accommodate in his thinking. Usually, in his confrontation with the modern world, he retreated into the past. But Hitler's past was constructed on the basis of a flawed history, an irrational history, rooted in his distinctly warped emotions. He seems to have believed that the most valuable blood, the foundation of a noble race, had been dispersed over the centuries and that it was his task to

reconstitute this blood-bank, and make it work, once again, for Germany's greatness. His racial laws, the eccentricities of the Nazi regime — the Adolf Hitler schools, the *Ordensburgen* — castles which were to resemble those of a medieval military order, where a new type of man was to be bred and educated — the concept of the SS as the guardians of the new order, were based on that belief, and so were the complementary anti-semitic measures.

Hitler's second obsession derived from his concern with *Lebensraum*. The new man, fearless and cruel, partly a descendant of Nietzsche's blond beast, who would no longer suffer from the 'sickness of mixed, corrupt blood', would need more space where he could act out Hitler's fantasies. He would have to be able to draw on sources of food and raw materials, and he could not be accommodated by a society where 140 people were crowded into one square kilometre. The thought of such density of population haunted Hitler. The *Lebensraum* problem of a tightly packed industrial society could not be solved by expansion overseas or the setting up of colonies. Neither Hitler nor any of his close associates, despite their discovery of the new academic discipline of geopolitics, were able to take a broad, global view of the international scene. The solid racial nucleus would have to find a new, expanded home for itself on the continent of Europe, and

perhaps Eurasia: the historic German *Drang nach Osten*, the breakthrough to the East, would be resumed.

Hitler as 'philosopher' was not an easy subject for the satirist and political cartoonist to tackle, even in the Goebbels-controlled magazine *Simplicissimus*. On 14 July 1935 there was an oblique reference here to the puzzle put to old-fashioned thinkers by the concept of 'new Europe'. In a drawing by Gulbransson entitled *Decline of the West?* the artist used the following text: 'In the shadow of his cares the philosopher contemplates matters of the future, without noticing that in the meanwhile a new Europe has begun to emerge.' More directly, the connection

ANTONÍN PELC was born in Líšany in Czechoslovakia in 1895. He studied painting and drawing at the Czech Academy in Prague and for a time took part in the Cubist movement. His political cartoons appeared in the leading Czech daily papers and in satirical magazines. He consistently and vigorously attacked the Nazis, and together with Hoffmeister, Bidlo and others took part in the Mánes exhibition in Prague in 1934. Together with Hoffmeister, he left Prague after its occupation by the Germans and went to the USA where he survived the war.

Nomination for 1938, Charles G. Werner, *Daily Oklahoman*, 1938 (right) and *What, No Chair for Me?*, David Low, *Evening Standard*, 30 September 1938 (below)
In connection with the Czechoslovak crisis, American cartoonists have used a broader range of interpretations than the Europeans. The high quality of American reporting from Europe, and perhaps America's ethnic hinterland, helped their work. Low's cartoon on the ill-fated Munich Agreement highlights not so much the betrayal of the Czechs as the exclusion of Stalin from the conference. The four-power Munich pact, which Low has hidden under Hitler's chair, was a mere pawn in Hitler's game of political warfare.

| Hitler | Chamberlain | Daladier | Mussolini | Stalin |

WHAT, NO CHAIR FOR ME ?

What Next?, David Fitzpatrick, *St Louis Post-Dispatch*, 25 September 1938 (left)
Fitzpatrick's powerful drawing leaves no doubt about the inexorable march of the gigantic Nazi war machine. Crushed under its heavy wheels lies Czechoslovakia. Fitzpatrick's questioning title is full of fear and foreboding.

Keeping the Home Fires Burning, David Low, *Evening Standard*, 25 July 1938 (below)
There is little doubt in Low's mind about who was responsible for the Sudeten crisis.

Göbbels

KEEPING THE HOME FIRES BURNING

The Farce of Bayreuth, French
The German top brass with the aged President Hindenburg in their midst are taken aback by the suprise appearance of would-be Wagnerian hero, Hitler-Lohengrin.

between Hitler's twin *Blut und Boden* concern and Wagner's evocation of German myths was established in an anonymous French cartoon on the subject of the 'Farce of Bayreuth'.

Training for the 'leap to the great final goals', made by Hitler in World War II, had started some time before its outbreak. For over four hours on 5 November 1937, in a mood of exaltation, Hitler outlined his plans to a few men who came to a secret conference in Berlin. Von Neurath, the Foreign Minister, von Blomberg, the War Minister, von Fritsch, the army chief, Admiral Raeder, chief of the Navy, and Göring, the air force chief, were present, and the minutes of the meeting were kept by Colonel Hossbach. Hitler said that his statement was to be regarded as his testament in the event of his death, and that, if the body of the nation was to be safeguarded and preserved, then the problem of living space had to be confronted straightaway, or at the latest between 1943 and 1945. The incorporation of Austria and Czechoslovakia into the German Reich would have to come first, and he was convinced that England and France had already written off Czechoslovakia. Hitler was not content with the annexation of Sudetenland, the border areas of Czechoslovakia inhabited by the Germans, but intended a swift assault on the country to give him a springboard for further expansion. A sharp discussion of Hitler's exposition followed; Fritsch in particular,

together with Neurath and Blomberg were stunned by it and warned Hitler of the danger of war with the Western powers. Eventually, all the men who argued with Hitler at that conference disappeared from their posts; after the churches, the Foreign Ministry as well as the high command of the army were brought into line.

During the next four years, Hitler acquired and shed many diplomatic and military advantages and in the end manipulated Germany into an untenable strategic situation. Both Russia and America had played key roles in World War I: Russia by forcing Germany to fight on two fronts in the first phase of the war, America by restoring the balance in the West when the Russian front collapsed during the Revolution in 1917. From the time of the negotiation of the Franco-Soviet and Czechoslovak-Soviet pacts in 1935, Russia resumed her active role in European politics. But she was still regarded as a dubious ally and, when the British policy of appeasement got under way, there was no place for Russia in the scheme of things: in fact, antagonism to the Soviet regime was one of the main sources of that policy. In Britain, working for the London *Evening Standard*, David Low was an eloquent advocate of British cooperation with the Soviet Union, and a sharp critic of the policy of appeasement. He later wrote in his autobiography that his cartoons against Hitlerism started in 1923, though he did not know

Hit and Muss on Their Axis, David Low (above)
Goebbels' objection to Low's irreverent portrayal of Hitler and Mussolini in these roles caused a diplomatic incident. Low repeats the 'windbag' image here that he had used earlier in describing Hitler and includes his new Axis partner, Japan.

The Key, Bert Strube, *Daily Express*, 17 February 1938 (left)
The day before, Austria had announced the formation — under Nazi pressure — of a new cabinet that included the Viennese Nazi Seyss-Inquart as Minister of the Interior. Only a few weeks later Austria's Anschluss with Germany was consummated.

it: 'One of my general themes then was that if the victorious democracies carried on as though German democrats were as much the world's enemies as German Junkers, and if they did not foster and strengthen the new Weimar government instead of driving it to collapse, the wrong Germans must inevitably gain power.[4]

Low's contemptuous treatment of many democratic politicians misled Hitler into asking in 1930, as one artist to another, for a few of Low's original drawings to hang on the walls in the new Nazi party headquarters in Munich. Less than three years later the *Evening Standard* and all papers printing Low's cartoons were banned in Germany following the publication of his cartoon *It Worked at the Reichstag, Why Not Here?*, which implied that Hitler was capable of destroying the League of Nations in the same way as he destroyed the Reichstag. Having observed Hitler in political action after January 1933, Low found it impossible to regard him as a certifiable lunatic, as H.G. Wells for instance did, or as a mere windbag, which was frequently the view of Hitler the opposition took (Hitler is nothing but the noise he makes, in the words of Kurt Tucholsky). Low remarked of Hitler:

His political conceptions were the artist's conceptions, seen in shapes, laid on in wide sweeps, errors painted out and details left until later, the bold approach and no fumbling. Essentially a simple mind, uncomplicated by pity. The clever-clever political analysts were

deep-thinking the inner meaning of his words, imparting their own complexity of mind to the object of their attentions and writing about Hitler as through he were an inexplicable enigma. I assumed that he would do just as he said and made my comment accordingly, earning for myself a cheap reputation as a prophet of remarkable insight when now and then I got in a cartoon about an event well before it happened.[5]

Low annoyed the Nazi leaders so much that when Lord Halifax, the Foreign Secretary, visited Germany late in 1937, Goebbels whipped himself into a rage over Low's cartoons. When Halifax returned to London, Low was asked to lunch with him. He asked the Foreign Secretary whether he would 'find it easier to promote peace if my cartoons did not irritate the Nazis personally?' The answer was yes, and Low toned down, for the time being, his comments on the personalities of the Nazi leaders. He replaced his strip cartoon, *Hit and Muss* with a new character called Muzzler, who incorporated features of both dictators. Low, who believed that Halifax had been taken for a ride by Hitler and Goebbels, was amazed by the sheep-like docility of well-meaning people. A writer in the *Church Times*, for instance, commented that 'Good taste, an element of which is kindness, forbids joking concerning subjects which are held sacred by others . . . I doubt whether Low's cartoons make Mr Chamberlain's appeasement path any easier.'

Wonder How Long the Honeymoon
Will Last?, Clifford Berryman,
9 October 1939 (right);
Rendezvous, David Low, Evening
Standard, 20 September 1939
(below); Hitler and Stalin, Kem,
1940 (below right)
The pact between Stalin and Hitler
fascinated and puzzled
cartoonists. Low shows them
meeting over the dead body of
Poland after the lightning
occupation of the country.

WONDER HOW LONG THE HONEYMOON WILL LAST?

Hitler   **RENDEZVOUS**   Stalin

POLAND.—LEBENSRAUM FOR THE CONQUERED

Poland — Lebensraum for the Conquered, David Low, *Evening Standard,* 20 January 1940 (above)
Low's grim cartoon depicts the 'resettlement' of Polish nationals and Jews to the 'living space' of the barren region of Lublin, east of Cracow. The hounding of Poles and Jews from their own homes and their deportation was ostensibly carried out to make room for the Germans of foreign nationality who were pouring into the Reich from all over Europe. Within a year some 1,200,000 Poles and 300,000 Jews were driven east.

Der Fuchs und der Igel.
Eine Tierfabel nach Lafontaine

Es sprach der Fuchs zum Igel klein:
„Vertrau mir, zieh die Stacheln ein,
Nie hätt ich dich gebissen!
Du störst den Frieden ohne Not,
Ich fühle mich direkt bedroht,
Ich wollt' dich ja nur – küssen!"

Low's pre-war cartoons advocating cooperation with the Soviet Union did more than merely reflect his left-wing inclinations. Low had visited the Soviet Union, and there he found out that the cartoonist Boris Efimov of *Izvestia* and his colleague on *Pravda* were paid 6,000 roubles a month, four times the official salary of Stalin. He also learned that they kept criticism of Stalin's regime to themselves. About the time of the Munich agreement Low became convinced that Britain and France would have to have Russia and America with them if Hitler forced war. His cartoons chronicle the relations between the Soviet Union and western democracies, and between the Soviet Union and Germany. They also advocated a policy which was unpopular with the appeasers, thereby contributing, in a small way, to their undoing.

On 12 March 1938 German troops invaded Austria in a smooth, co-ordinated military operation, preceded by diplomatic bullying. In Goebbels' words Austria was not a nation but a hallucination; it ceased to exist, and Hitler's *Grossdeutschland* became a reality. Austria 'returned to the Reich', an act which was outlawed by the peace treaties. Most Austrians were jubilant, although in the first night after the occupation some 67,000 people were arrested in Vienna alone.

In the spring of 1938, Germany's pressure on

Czechoslovakia to meet the claims of Sudeten Germans grew to a point where the Prague government ordered mobilization. Britain and France urged the Czechs to meet German claims and the declaration, in Moscow, that the Soviet Union would meet its obligations to Czechoslovakia and to France was ignored.

The Russians kept a close watch on affairs: they knew that in both Britain and France there were many admirers of Hitler and Mussolini, as well as fascist parties with strong press backing. In government circles in London and Paris, a conservative Germany was regarded as a bulwark against communism; that attitude, combined with Hitler's frequent assertion that Germany must expand to the East, had far-reaching and alarming implications for Moscow.

Apart from its anti-Soviet aspect, the policy of appeasement rested on the view that Germany had been short-changed in the peace treaties. Hitler learned to profit from that view. In the international crisis before the outbreak of the war, German nationalism, in its Nazi form, was presented as an ineluctable reality, a vital force which had to be satisfied. At Munich Czechoslovakia lost its border areas and fortifications and most of its German citizens, which left the country indefensible. Heartfield used the fable of the hedgehog and the fox to illustrate its position. The Czech hedgehog, bristling with

Beck   Chamberlain   Litvinov
A PIECE MISSING, TOVARISH

This Time He Left Me His Umbrella, Jean Effel, September 1938
(far left)
*Chamberlain had in effect 'left behind' a carte blanche to seize
Czechoslovakia.*

The Fox and the Hedgehog, John Heartfield, 1938 (left)
*Heartfield based his comment on the Sudeten crisis on
La Fontaine's fable about the fox and the hedgehog.*

A Piece Missing, Tovarish, David Low, *Evening Standard*,
5 April 1939 (above)
*Low's cartoon was drawn only a few days after the
Anglo-French guarantee to Poland was announced. The Soviet
Union was not a party to it.*

Take Me to Czechoslovakia, Driver, Vaughn Shoemaker,
Chicago Daily News, 1938 (right)
*This is one of Shoemaker's most successful drawings, with
Hitler being driven by the figure of death.*

TAKE ME TO CZECHOSLOVAKIA, DRIVER

small arms faced the fox; the big guns were
behind the fox, who told the hedgehog: 'Trust me,
draw in your needles, I would never bite you! You
disturb peace without cause, I feel directly
threatened, and all I want to do is to kiss you!' In
America, Fitzpatrick commented on the inexorable
advances by Hitler's Germany in *What
Next?* (p. 95).

Though Hitler declared, in writing, that the
acquisition of Sudetenland satisfied his territorial
demands, and Chamberlain announced, on his
return to London, 'peace in our time', there was
worse to come. On 15 March 1939 German armies
marched into Prague. By then the concept of
'collective security' against aggression — Maxim
Litvinov, the Soviet Foreign Minister, was one of its
leading supporters and by this stage Britain gave
guarded support to the notion — had been
severely damaged. The cartoon *A Piece Missing,
Tovarish* shows Litvinov showing the gap in
collective security to Chamberlain and to the
Polish Minister of Foreign Affairs, Beck.

Early in April 1939, Nazi propaganda turned to
Poland with demands for the return of Danzig and
of the Polish corridor. Chamberlain and Deladier
then gave guarantees to Poland and Rumania. The
Soviet Union refused to underwrite the guarantees
and, instead, Litvinov asked for an alliance with
Britain and France. Chamberlain hesitated,
because he did not want to provoke Hitler. When,

two months later, negotiations for a Triple Alliance
opened in Moscow, Stalin had reviewed the Soviet
position. Litvinov had been replaced by Molotov,
who was suspicious of the intentions of the
western powers. The negotiators, Foreign
Secretary Halifax, his East Europe expert William
Strang and Maisky, the Soviet Ambassador to
London who belonged to the Litvinov school of
Soviet foreign policy, could not persuade Molotov
to opt for the treaty. Molotov had already had talks
in Berlin, and Soviet conditions had become
tougher. They included a free hand in the Baltic
states as well as the right of the Red Army to
march through Poland, a point which the Poles did
not want to concede. Molotov was reluctant to be
pinned down by the Triple Alliance.

The Nazi-Soviet Pact was signed on 23 August
— eight days before Hitler's forces marched into
Poland — and arranged for a partition of Poland
between Russia and Germany. Low's cartoon of
20 September 1939 contrasted the new polite
posture of Stalin and Hitler with their past abuse of
each other (p. 98). In a particularly grim cartoon,
Low described the implementation of Hitler's
Lebensraum policy in the East: the plan for
conquered Poland included the recruitment of
Polish POWs for Germany's war industries and
the resettlement of Polish Jews in the barren area
around Lublin (p. 99).

Jekyll and Hyde, Bernard Partridge, *Punch*, 17 April 1940

War: The Ultimate Goal

In 1944, David Low wrote:

If Hitler has not succeeded in establishing his 'New Order' in Europe, certainly he has established the United Nations of cartoonists. Today throughout the free world the work of graphic satirists bears a recognisable family likeness. Already, before the war, uniform methods of reproduction had gone far to impose a conventional form and technique of presentation, but it remained for a uniting event to inspire a similar outlook. Hitler supplied the event. Now, despite tags and titles in foreign script (which can be guessed at, usually) the cartoons of the civilised nations have become virtually interchangeable . . . they reflect the common approach to the one subject-matter of the day — war against Nazi Germany[1].

There was indeed much traffic in ideas and techniques during the war: the outcome of such traffic was a highly homogenized picture of Hitler and of his Germany. Hitler himself had been on the international scene long enough for his act to become familiar; one or two other Nazi leaders — Göring and Goebbels — had also had their measure taken. Heinrich Himmler, the police chief, joined the top rank of Nazi leaders during the war; his reflection in caricature, therefore, was hardly visible before 1939. Artists preferred illustrating events rather than analysing the nature of the Nazi regime or the character of Hitler. In contrast with the early, subtle dissection of Hitler's standing in society by George Grosz, his treatment by cartoonists during the war was much rougher. It was sufficient to sketch his moustache, clipped short, and his forelock, hinting at some bohemian, non-military past. The trick was simple, and could equally serve the purpose of presenting Hitler as a fiend or a fool. Had he had any choice in the matter, Hitler would have preferred the former view of himself, but more often, he was presented as a fool.

Even some of his associates thought Hitler to be of a pathologically militant nature; war was for him the 'strongest and most classic manifestation of politics', the ultimate goal of politics. It was his conviction that a long period of peace would do untold harm to the nation; war, not peace, he saw as the natural condition of man. World War I shaped Hitler and his generation: many of them remained fascinated by war, by hostility, by bloodshed, and peace was for them an unpleasant and dull state of affairs. War was, for Hitler, chiefly a way of acquiring territory, and he came near to formulating the idea of a permanent war. As the power and territory of Germany was extended, it would keep on coming up against new frontiers, which would provide fresh conflicts. In that way, Hitler believed, the new German race would be hardened.

As for the result of the war, Hitler thought in terms of extreme alternatives. Victory, glory and a much-improved life would come out of a

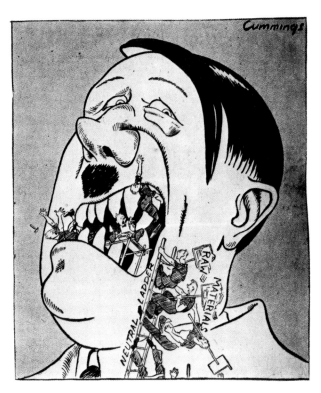

NEW RULER OF THE WORLD

successful war; annihilation, disaster and death would follow failure. A simple, unrealistic view, perhaps rooted in Hitler's own warped personality, it was remote from the complexities of war and peace in the twentieth century. By 1939 it was clear that Hitler was trying to discard the ambiguities of politics; on his way to power, then in the process of putting Germany under his control, and in his foreign political moves he had acted as a cautious pirate who never neglected to exploit opportunities for piracy. The war, with its stark alternatives, released him from such ambiguities.[2] Hitler moved away from tactical flexibility to rigid attitudes; ideology replaced policies.

Though Hitler's political personality was an anachronism in the twentieth century, there was nothing out of date about the technical instruments with which Hitler's Germany conducted the war. Massive commitment of tanks, with air support, was a design for mobility, in contrast with the static trench warfare of World War I. The mechanized nature of modern warfare formed the background for several drawings by Fitzpatrick in America: for instance, the inexorable mechanical swastika in his *What Next?* cartoon (see page 95). David Low was another cartoonist who used mechanized war and its requirements, in his drawing *The Iron Comes Back*. The iron, which the Norwegians had been selling to Germany,

returned with an army of occupation.

Hitler desired war and he provoked it; there was no question in 1939 — as there had been in 1914 — of a shared war guilt. But Germany was not ready for it — or at least not ready for a war against Britain and France, in addition to Poland — in September 1939. There were no cheering crowds in Berlin, as there had been in August 1914. Only about a half of Hitler's 102 divisons were ready for battle; the navy did not achieve the strength allowed it in the Anglo-German Naval Pact, and was inferior to both the British and French navies. The air force alone, with its 3,298 planes on the eve of the war, was stronger than the enemy forces. Ammunition stocks and troop equipment were low, and Germany had to import most of its strategic materials such as bauxite, tin, oil and copper (99 per cent, 80 per cent, 75 per cent and 70 per cent respectively). Those weaknesses forced on Germany certain ways of conducting the war: a *Blitzkrieg* against selected isolated targets rather than a long and continuous war against the enemy alliance. Even in the early stages of the war, Hitler's belief in his own infallibility was apparent; only artists, he said, could become great generals.

Nevertheless, in October 1939, after Poland's swift defeat, Hitler found himself in a situation he had misread. He had misread the attitude of Britain and France shortly before the beginning of the

NORWAY
IRON ORE
FOR EXPORT

THE IRON COMES BACK

war, and he thought that after Poland's subjugation, Britain at least would see the error of her ways, or that Stalin might bring Russia into the war on Germany's side. Later, in March 1940, Hitler thought that the decision would come in France where the *Sitzkrieg*, the phony war in the West, was about to become the *Blitzkrieg*. The war in the West was for him a detour before launching an offensive against the East. Though it took almost two years before Hitler ordered his armed forces to invade Russia, leaving the war in the West unfinished and Britain undefeated, the eastward move was his primary objective. There was a continuity, in his mind, between the first and second World War: on 23 November 1939 he said 'Today the second act of the drama is being written.' The drive for more living space and the fear of bolshevik revolutionary menace came conveniently together: Hitler, a small-part actor in the first war had the stage to himself in the second. In both wars, expansionist policy in the East was the key to Germany's world hegemony. Hitler's Austrian origins and early life helped him to understand the east European implications of Germany's imperialist policy; after the 1917 revolution in Russia, central and west European anxieties over the communist threat made Germany's *Drang nach Osten* appear not unattractive. But Hitler, like his predecessors in World War I, was careless about exposing

Germany to a war on two fronts, and he underestimated the resilience of the British.

The war, of course, focused the attention of cartoonists. At the centre of the target, in visual terms, there was Hitler with his moustache and forelock. Around him were deployed the mechanical instruments of destruction: the expressionless monsters born out of the technology of the modern industrial state. Yet, on the whole, cartoonists tended to ignore the technological hardware of modern war; their task was perhaps more difficult than, say, Goya's had been, because, unlike him, they rarely saw at first hand the suffering of the ordinary man. Their art became less subtle and more hard-hitting and as the appeal to patriotic emotions became stronger, the propaganda element in caricature came to the forefront. Artists felt obliged to do their patriotic duty and this became especially marked when they turned to the home front. They used up their fund of mockery on the enemy: at home they explained, or celebrated. In this respect, the political truce on the home front subtly changed, in their own societies, the outlook and standing of cartoonists.

Artists whose stock-in-trade was irreverence temporarily abandoned their former attitudes. Churchill had just formed a national government including both Labour and Liberal members and promised the British a future involving 'blood, sweat and tears'. Before the German offensive in

*The Invincible Morale
of the People,* Clive
Upton, *Daily Sketch,*
7 September 1940
(right)
This cartoon conveys
the intense patriotic
mood of the British
people in one of their
darkest hours (British
aircraft losses at this
time were exceeding
their production) and
suggests that the
Luftwaffe would fail to
win the battle of the
air.

Harvest Moon, David
Low, *Evening
Standard,* 9 May 1941
(below)
The invention of radar
made the Luftwaffe's
moonlight attacks on
England increasingly
expensive.

HARVEST MOON

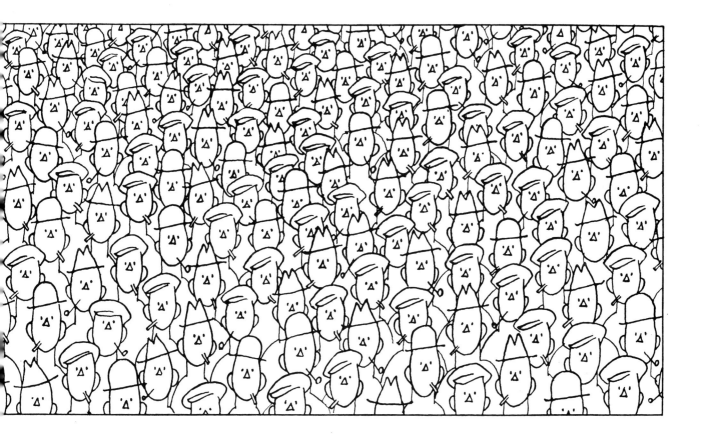

The Changing Face of Britain, Fougasse, *Punch*, 17 January 1940
Fougasse (Cyril Kenneth) plainly shows the general mobilization of Britain.

MARDI-GRAS

Le Masque

The Mask, anon., *Mardi-Gras*, 24 February 1941
(above)
*Although Laval had not yet become premier of
France, his collaboration with Hitler and the Nazis
was perfectly clear to the author of this drawing.
No doubt the caricaturist in occupied France
preferred to remain anonymous.*

the West was launched on 10 May 1940 and the
phony war was concluded, and during the Battle of
Britain, the Luftwaffe, the air force, was Hitler's
main instrument for conducting the war. Its
commander-in-chief, Hermann Göring, said in
1940, 'My Luftwaffe is invincible. Just look at its
achievements in Poland and in France — can one
conceive of a war machine in history which has
contributed so much towards such total victories
as these. As a fighting force surely the Luftwaffe is
a living monument to National Socialism . . . And so
now we turn to England. How long will this one last
— two, three weeks? Our bombers will make short
work of the little islanders.'[3] In fact, the Luftwaffe
failed to acquire and maintain control of the air in
Europe. Göring regarded it mainly as an offensive
tactical weapon. Defensive fighters and heavy
aircraft for strategic bombing were less well
developed, to the ultimate cost of Germany's war
effort.

The weaknesses of Germany's air force was
apparent in the Battle of Britain. Its task was no
longer to support fast-moving tanks and infantry in
a *Blitzkrieg*, but to destroy the RAF as well as
break the morale of the British people before the
invasion. It almost succeeded in its first task. In the
last two weeks of August and the first week of
September 1940, British losses of fighter aircraft
exceeded their production; many airfields in
south-east England were bombed and fighter pilot

casualties were at almost a quarter of total force.
Early in September the Germans were deflected
from their struggle with the RAF, and concentrated
on the destruction of London and of British aircraft
factories. But in this manoeuvre the Luftwaffe were
weak compared, with, say, the Allied strategic
bombing offensive in 1944. Germany's air offensive
against Britain was suspended in May 1941, when
only four bomber squadrons out of the original
forty-four were still operational. By then, however,
most of the Luftwaffe potential had been switched
to the East, and Britain survived as the only base in
the West for a continued campaign against Hitler's
Germany.

Many cartoonists portrayed the unbroken will of
the British to continue the fight. Fougasse made a
telling point subtly in his *Changing Face of Britain*
(p. 107). About the time when Germany's air
offensive against Britain was ending, David Low
drew the cartoon *Harvest Moon* (p. 106). It
contained an oblique reference to the invention
and use of radar, which made it possible for the
RAF to inflict heavy losses on the Luftwaffe during
night raids. By then, most of western Europe was
under German occupation, including half of
France. Adolf Hoffmeister portrayed Laval as a
procuress inviting Hitler to despoil the other half.

Though Hitler's position in central and western
Europe was strong early in 1941, it was vulnerable.
In addition, the various quislings and their regimes

Mrs Laval, Matchmaker, Adolf Hoffmeister, 1943 (left)
Hoffmeister depicts Laval as a brothel madame, displaying to Hitler the charms of a stripped but still unready France. At the end of 1942 the treacherous Laval had, indeed, encouraged Hitler's plans for the total occupation of France.

Family Group, Stephen Roth (right)
Roth's legend to this group portrait of Hitler's allies and collaborators is: 'Let's have a family group photograph, children — Heaven knows whether we will be together next year.' The group includes Marshal Mannerheim of Finland, Mussolini, Quisling of Norway, Laval, Boris of Bulgaria, Horthy of Hungary and the Slovak Tiso.

in occupied Europe were operating from an insecure political base. In that situation, Hitler's attention turned to the East. In a conversation with Field Marshal von Bock in February 1941, when he was told that the Russians could sustain heavy defeats without making peace, Hitler replied in an off-hand way that, after the conquest of the Ukraine, Moscow and Leningrad, the Soviets would 'certainly consent to a compromise'. Hitler invaded Yugoslavia and Greece in April 1941; on 22 June, Russia was attacked on a front some 2,000 miles long. The Balkan operation caused the dangerous postponement of the assault on the Soviet Union by four weeks. It was probably a fatal delay. It is likely that Hitler was aware of the weakness of his position. The danger for Germany of a war on two fronts, in the East and in the West, had been clearly shown in World War I. Military deficiencies in Mussolini's Italy had become apparent in the African and the Balkan campaigns so that relations between Hitler and Mussolini deteriorated and came to resemble relations between master and servant, rather than between allies.

But, in the spring of 1941, Hitler would not consider the possibility of Germany's defeat. Swift victory in the East would make it easy for him to deal with Britain. For Hitler the summer of 1941 offered the last chance of completing his grand design. A long-drawn war of attrition, however,

would make Germany increasingly dependent on raw materials from Russia. Hitler probably wanted to anticipate such development. He underestimated the military potential of the Soviet Union as much as he overestimated Germany's potential; he was convinced the Germany was safe in the West, and that he would be committing a crime against the German nation if he did not seize the opportunity of attacking Russia. The Nazi-Soviet Pact, which, Hitler said, 'was never honestly intended', would cease to exist. A loud sigh of relief was audible in all Nazi propaganda directives soon after the launching of the Russian campaign: the unwelcome restraint with regard to hated *Bolschewismus* could at last be given up.

A week after the invasion, Goebbels gave spirited instructions to the German press:

Reports from the whole of Europe against Bolshevism can be noted, such as were never observed until now. Europe marches against the common enemy in a unique solidarity, and rises, as it were, against the oppressor of all human culture and civilization. This hour of birth of the new Europe is being accomplished without any demand or pressure from the German side. On the contrary, it is clear that even the small and the smallest states have understood the common European task, since they have called up their sons to make a blood sacrifice for the common idea. For this reason we do not want to speak of a crusade. Newspapers are faced here with an immense task, as it is essential, especially in

Belgium Revisited, David Low, *Evening Standard,* 16 May 1940 (below) and *Vot You Mean — You Think You Don't Know Nodding About It!* Giles, *Evening Standard,* 9 May 1941 (right)
The sparkling humour of Giles's cartoon provides comic relief from the reality of Holland's fate in 1940.

110

Melancholia, Antonin Pelc, 1943 (left)
By the beginning of 1943 the Italian forces had been defeated in North Africa, Mussolini himself was ill and disillusioned and defeatism was rife among the Italian people. Although Hitler still declared that the 'voice of history beckoned them', Mussolini had reached the end of the line. Pelc shows a Hamlet-like Hitler contemplating the grave and skull of his old ally.

His Master's Voice, Trier (above)
Trier's effective cartoon shows the Italian dictator as nothing more than Hitler's doleful mouthpiece.

Превращение фрицев

regard to America, that the unity of Europe in the fight against Bolshevism is made clear to the new world as well. The great hour has also come for the settling of accounts with the English claptrap and thesis that Adolf Hitler is a dictator, who rushes restlessly from country to country like a modern Genghis Khan, because one aggression forces him into other [aggressions]. Adolf Hitler has proved himself to be the military leader of Europe on behalf of its common culture and civilization, and is recognized as such by the whole European world.[4]

Finnish, Hungarian, Slovak, Italian and Rumanian units took part in the Russian campaign; they were later joined by volunteers from Spain, Belgium, France, Holland and Norway. But Hitler's *Wehrmacht* bore the brunt of the campaign: Boris Efimof made that point in a drawing for *Krokodil*, the Moscow satirical magazine. In a cartoon which appeared on 7 July 1941, David Low contrasted 'Russian treachery' with Hitler's claim to represent European civilization. Though the Germans swiftly pushed far into Russia, they failed, by Christmas 1941, to capture Leningrad and Moscow: in order to restore confidence at home, Hitler announced that he would take over high command of the armed forces, so that they would have the direct benefit of his powers of intuition. David Low commented on Hitler's 'sleep-walking' qualities in a strong drawing (p. 114) entitled *In Future the Army Will Be Guided by My Intuitions.* Fitzpatrick's

attitude on the new situation was interestingly divided. On the one hand, he perceived the need of a strong Russian war effort against the invaders; on the other, he could not quite believe his eyes when he considered the new partnership between Britain and Russia (p.115).

Probably the most successful propaganda device used in the war was Churchill's V for Victory sign. The motif was repeated in the signature tune of BBC broadcasts to occupied Europe, in the form of the opening bars from Beethoven's Fifth Symphony, the three short notes and one long suggesting the letter V in the Morse alphabet. Goebbels and the Nazi leaders were worried about the impact of the V device and the frequency with which it appeared, in its visual and musical form, in occupied Europe. Goebbels tried to turn the device around by pretending that it stood for Viktoria, an unidentified German goddess of victory, or Caesar's triumphant *veni, vidi, vici* and the victory of Germany against Bolshevism.

Of all the artists working during the war, David Low was probably the most effective interpreter of the German home front. The art of the German and many other Continental artists did not prosper in exile. John Heartfield, for instance, who spent the war in London, produced a few photomontages but they were less powerful and more derivative than his earlier work. David Low's touch was more certain and he did not hesitate to deal with

Hitler's Allies, Boris Efimov, 1942 (far left)
The motley volunteer troops from occupied western Europe as well as from Spain, the Italians and the soldiers of the various satellite countries, were not only scruffy, but less than enthusiastic in their support of the Reich.

The Conversion of the Fritzes, Kukriniksy, 1941-2 (left)
Hitler's decision to hold territory at any cost was quickly breeding a new 'white army' of the Third Reich — the dead buried under the Russian snow.

Russian Treachery, David Low, *Evening Standard*, 9 July 1941 (right)
Hitler invaded the USSR on 22 June 1941; he believed then that the Nazi war machine would secure victory in three months. Low comments on how Hitler's initial advance proved unexpectedly costly, although the Russians did fall back.

RUSSIAN TREACHERY

Germany's home front. In the summer of 1942, in particular, Low drew several cartoons which showed his mastery of the theme. He pointed to the dependence of Germany's war industries on foreign labour in *How Much for This Lot?* (p. 119) drawn on 6 July. The behaviour of the German forces of occupation deteriorated as they spread to the European east: in Russia, it was barbaric. Himmler was given the responsibility to supervise 'special tasks' in the theatre of operations, arising from the 'conflicts of two opposing political systems'. Jews, Communist Party functionaries, gypsies and 'Asiatic inferiors' were to be exterminated. A propaganda drive against Slav 'sub-humans' *(Untermenschen)* was launched; members of the armed forces were made exempt from prosecution for crimes against the civilian population. Political commissars of the Red Army were to be shot out of hand, and Bolshevism was presented as the worst threat from the steppe since Genghis Khan. In Moscow, Boris Efimov portrayed Himmler as 'The Spider' (see page 63); in London in December 1942, David Low informed his readers of the fate of the Jews. Methods of mass extermination, first used by the Nazis in the Russian campaign, were applied in the course of Hitler's 'final solution' of the Jewish problem.

Some months after Hitler's attack on Russia, on 7 December 1941, 350 Japanese planes launched from aircraft carriers attacked the American fleet at Pearl Harbor. Four days later, Hitler declared war on the United States, the war he had previously regared with foreboding. There had been competition for America's favours earlier in the war, but many Americans drew back from involvement in the traditional, often incomprehensible animosities of Europe. Fitzpatrick exemplified that distrust; early in 1941, intervention in Europe seemed to him to be a lethal adventure.

The invasion of Russia and America's entry into the war in 1941 marked the turning point of the war. It has been argued[5] that the decision to declare war on America contained an element of recognition, on Hitler's part, that his design for the war had failed. Germany derived a marginal advantage from the decision: at sea, the German navy could wage war without restraint. But the fact could not be concealed that, in two years, Hitler had lost a position of military and political advantage and faced an unbeatable combination of states. In the following year, the superiority of the alliance began to show. At the end of October 1942, the second battle of Alamein turned the tide for the British in Africa. However, the eastern front was still Hitler's obsession as it had been since the end of 1941 to the exclusion of other theatres of war. For Hitler the war on the eastern front was an ideological war as well as an old-fashioned war of expansion. Hitler did not aim

Drumming to Moscow,
Kukriniksy, 1942 (right)
*This caricature compares
Hitler's confident advance on
Moscow in September 1941
with his humiliating retreat in
December of the same year.
Beating the blitzkrieg drum
and certain that the Russian
people would overthrow
Stalin, the 'blitzkrieg drum' is
hurled back at Hitler by
Russia and bursts on his
head.*

*In Future the Army Will Be
Guided by My Intuitions,*
David Low, *Evening Standard,*
23 December 1941 (below
right)
*Hitler took over the High
Command himself. Low uses
Hitler's much flaunted, but by
now somewhat discredited,
'powers of intuition' to
indicate the disastrous effect
his direct leadership would
have on his sorely tried
generals and military
advisors.*

"IN FUTURE THE ARMY WILL B
GUIDED BY MY INTUITIONS

Society Item, David Fitzpatrick, *St Louis Post-Dispatch*, 9 July 1941 (left)
Fitzpatrick executed this drawing only a few days before the Anglo-Soviet Mutual Assistance agreement was signed. The stiffness of the poses and the title of the drawing suggest that Fitzpatrick regards it as an 'arranged' union.

Very Much Alive!, Philip Zec, *Daily Mirror*, 17 July 1941 (below left)
Zec's cartoon appeared two days before the BBC announced the existence of Resistance forces in Europe. Hitler, sitting on the coffin of France, is startled to see a hand emerge, writing V for Victory on the wall.

Glorifying the Führer, Kukriniksy (left)
Kukriniksy depicts Goebbels' attempts to keep the myth of the Führer's invincibility alive, a role increasingly difficult after 1943.

Stalingrad, Kukriniksy, 1943 (right) and *Gateway to Stalingrad*, David Fitzpatrick, *St Louis Post-Dispatch*, 25 November 1942 (far right)
Kukriniksy uses the text 'There is a cliff on the Volga' to describe Russian resistance to the attack on Stalingrad. Despite military intelligence and the advice of his generals, Hitler, by now increasingly cut off from reality, would not give up. Fitzpatrick's devastating drawing, reminiscent of Weber's most powerful works, sums up the disaster.

to acquire colonies overseas, but he attacked instead one of the great European powers, and its destruction was his aim.

Seen in this context, every other battlefront played a subordinate role for Hitler, and gradually he lost interest in them. His headquarters were positioned behind the eastern front; before the beginning of the summer 1942 campaign, Hitler transferred his headquarters from Rastenburg in East Prussia to Vinnitsa in the Ukraine. Here, he defended his decisions to push on to the Caucasus and capture Stalingrad, against the advice of his generals. He even disputed matters of hard intelligence: he refused to believe the fact that Russia's production of tanks was running at 1,200 units a month, dismissing it as 'idiotic nonsense'. He became increasingly withdrawn and isolated at the nerve-centre of Germany's war effort in the East, and his behaviour became more overtly pathological. He began to eat his meals alone, accompanied only by his Alastian dog; the daily conferences with his generals were gradually becoming more contentious, and careful minutes of them were taken; Hitler sometimes left the block-house where he lived for lonely walks at night along concealed paths. Hitler's headquarters, combined with the High Command of Germany's armed forces, were a mixture of monastery and concentration camp; a visitor noted there the 'smell of kitchens, uniforms, heavy boots.'

It was at Vinnitsa that Hitler and the generals watched the unfolding of the Stalingrad disaster. The Germans knew of Stalin's Order of the Day, simply stating that no more Russian soil must be surrendered to the enemy, so the conquest of Stalingrad became a matter of prestige for Hitler, who regarded the town as a kind of shrine of communism. As early as 24 August 1942 the *Wehrmacht* High Command made an urgent request to the press not to anticipate the early fall of Stalingrad, but to concern itself with the opening of the battle only. On 17 September the newspapers were informed that the battle for Stalingrad was approaching its victorious conclusion. The battle in fact raged on for four months; by the end of January 1943 von Paulus' Sixth Army was exhausted and demoralized, and on 2 February it surrendered to the Russians. In Moscow, Kukriniksy — the composite name of three graphic artists, Mikhail Kuprianov, Porfiri Krylov and Nikolai Sokolov — celebrated the Stalingrad victory in *There is a Cliff on the Volga*. In America, Fitzpatrick hailed the defeat of Hitler's armies in a powerful cartoon, reminiscent of Paul Weber's earlier drawings.

The public image of Hitler suffered a deterioration parallel with the disintegration of his personality. His former political charisma faded, and his magnetism declined along with his run of successes. The absence of striking, seemingly

effortless victories, diminished his powers of oratory; his appearances at the Sportpalast on 30 September 1942 and then again on 8 November at the Hofbräukeller in Munich revealed a leader whose spell had been broken. From the end of 1942, Goebbels did his utmost to fill the gap left by Hitler. He used the approach of Churchill's early speeches, giving pessimistic propaganda which promised the Germans nothing and asked them for even more effort. Many cartoons appeared in the Allied press on that theme. Nevertheless, Goebbels remained faithful to his creation: the Hitler myth. Certain adjustments had to be made. For the last time, Hitler was paraded before the Germans as 'utterly great' but also 'utterly lonely'. He was still working as hard as ever (an essential part of the myth) though by the time he was fifty-four years old in April 1943, 'indelible furrows on his face' had been sketched in by long days of work and endless nights without sleep. The difficulty of this refloating of the Hitler myth was portrayed by Kukriniksy.

Though the western allies — America and Britain — and the Soviet Union were drawing closer together in the years 1942 and 1943, the Russians never quite got over their pre-war suspicions that the western democracies had wanted to save themselves by diverting Hitler's ambitions towards the East. In June 1942 Roosevelt agreed with Molotov that there was a need for a second front in the West, a policy which conflicted with Churchill's preference for the 'soft underbelly' in the south of Europe. David Low summed up the problem in his drawing *What News from the Second Front?* (p. 118) and, more than a year later, in *Basic Winstonese.* Between October 1942 and May 1943 the Allied troops threw out the Germans and the Italians from North Africa and then invaded Sicily and Italy. On 3 September 1943 the Italians made a separate peace. The plight of the Nazi leaders was summed up in Vicky's drawing in the *News Chronicle* (p. 120).

After Stalingrad, and his differences with the generals, Hitler became even more of a recluse. Goebbels commented on his inclination to brood and his distaste for taking exercise. The atmosphere at his headquarters in the East was extremely depressing. When he was in company, which was now provided mainly by his secretaries, doctors and adjutants, Hitler's monologues were even longer, more insanely uncontrolled and more disregarding of his audience than before. In a way, Hitler returned to the habits of his youth; he became withdrawn, mentally unstable and alienated from his environment. When the forces of a large part of the globe were turned against him, Hitler reverted to the role of a local party leader. He was uncertain, suspicious, and his overwrought nerves sought release in explosive outbursts of rage.

What News from the Second Front?, David Low, *Evening Standard*, 14 July 1942 (right) and *Basic Winstonese*, David Low, *Evening Standard*, 27 September 1943 (below right)

Low shows the USSR's suspicions over the Allies' delay in setting up a second front in the West, as the hard-pressed Russian troops face yet another Nazi assault on their eastern borders. Churchill maintained that he was waiting for the right moment. By September 1943 when the balance of the war had changed he agreed to the establishment of a second front as soon as possible; in that month the Allies gained a foothold in Italy and the second front was finally established in June 1944 with the invasion of Normandy.

WHAT NEWS FROM THE SECOND FRONT?

BASIC WINSTONESE

How Much for This Lot?, David Low, *Evening Standard*, 6 July 1942 (left) and *I've Settled the Fate of Jews*, David Low, *Evening Standard*, 14 December 1942 (below left)

Again Low shows his sure touch when he deals with events in occupied Europe. This cartoon depicts the meeting of Ley, leader of the Nazi Labour Front, and Laval in Paris to discuss the Nazi demand for 150,000 workers to be sent to Germany to man the factories.

HOW MUCH FOR THIS LOT?

**"I'VE SETTLED THE FATE OF JEWS"—
"AND OF GERMANS"**

The Beggar's Opera

Vicky

Hitler took little notice of the suffering of the German civilian population during the severe strategic bombing carried out by the Allies in the second half of the war. Again, Goebbels and others had to stand in for Hitler. In July and August 1942 Hamburg was severely attacked by night and day seven times within nine days; the use of incendiary bombs caused the first firestorms and some 50,000 people were incinerated above and below ground. Berlin came under sixteen major attacks in four months in the winter of 1942–1943 by British bombers. Towards the end of the winter, the Americans, who concentrated on daytime raids, joined in. In the *Daily Herald,* George Whitelaw made a point about round-the-clock bombing. Though the civilian population suffered severe losses, strategic bombing neither broke its morale, nor did it succeed in destroying Germany's armament industry. Indeed, early in 1944 Germany's defences pushed Allied losses of bomber aircraft to 10 per cent, the highest casualties for any Allied arm in the war.

The fate of Hitler's Germany was settled by the advance of the land armies. The British and American forces established a foothold on the European mainland in Italy, in September 1943. A second front was finally established in the West when Normandy was invaded from the British base on 6 June 1944. After a tough campaign on the Italian peninsula, Allied armies had reached Rome two days before the operation in Normandy was opened. By August 1944, German forces had been expelled from the pre-war territory of the Soviet

---

DAVID LOW was born in Dunedin, New Zealand, in 1891. He was already contributing to a local newspaper by the age of 11 and at 17, despite his lack of formal training, became a full-time freelance artist. His cartoons first attracted attention when he was working for the *Bulletin* in Sydney, Australia, where he drew some highly successful and impudent cartoons of Billy Hughes, Australia's Labour premier. He went to London in 1919 to work and contributed to the *Star* until 1927 when he joined Lord Beaverbrook's *Evening Standard*. His most outstanding work appeared in the period before and during World War II when he was able to express his hatred of Hitler and the Nazi regime, and to comment on events in Europe in a number of astonishingly perceptive and powerfully drawn political cartoons. In 1953 he joined the *Guardian* to which he contributed regularly until his death in 1963. He was knighted in 1962. *Low's Autobiography* contains sharp comments on the caricaturist's art.

Round the Clock

Union. The defeat of Hitler's Germany was a matter of time. On 28 April 1945 the Allied and the Russian armies met on the river Elbe. By then, most of Berlin in the north and Vienna in the southeast had been occupied by the Russians, and Hitler had about two days to live.

There was little left of the Third Reich early in May 1945. A large gap in the range of subjects available to caricaturists was one of the unforeseen consequences of peace. The atom bomb, the East-West divide and later the consumer society temporarily filled some of the empty space. But a coherent campaign against inhumanity on the scale of the anti-Nazi campaign has not been mounted since the spring of 1945. Nor has the post-war decline of the newspapers as the main purveyor of the latest news helped the art of caricature.

In the campaign against Hitler and his creatures, caricature took a place of honour. In the first phase of that campaign, successive governments of the Weimar Republic allowed artists the freedom to attack and ridicule Hitler and his movement. During this period satire and caricature were used partly as a weapon against Hitler and the Nazis, partly as a sensitive instrument of political analysis. Not only did it illustrate the progress made by Hitler and his movement; it also pointed to their true nature. By 1934, detailed maps could have been drawn up of the

caricaturists' main targets.

But they had largely remained confined to Germany and other Central European countries. The campaign was gradually internationalized in the years before the war, reaching a global culmination during the war; its geographical broadening partly obliterated the earlier subtlety. Nevertheless, caricature provided a reliable commentary, or at least a description of Hitler's political progress, throwing sharp shafts of light into one of the darkest corners of European history.

German Autumn, Thomas Theodor Heine, 1944 (above)
Towards the end of his wartime exile, Heine drew this bitterly elegiac picture of the destruction of Germany.

House of Cards, David Low, *Evening Standard*, 25 August 1944 (right)
As Low shows, Hitler's 'new order' was collapsing as his satellite states, used and abused by him, were now unwilling or, as the Allies advanced, unable to lend him effective support.

Departure from Paris, Kukriniksy, 1944 (above right)
Kukriniksy picks on one of the more sordid aspects of the German evacuation of Paris. A German soldier, disguised as a French woman, is revealed as a looter.

Witnesses for the Prosecution, David Fitzpatrick, *St Louis Post-Dispatch*, 30 April 1945 (far right)
Fitzpatrick's deliberately bestial Nazi is confronted by the millions of dead the war has cost, all victims of Hitler's lust for conquest. The title refers to the trials of Nazi war criminals yet to come.

HOUSE OF CAR

WITNESSES FOR THE PROSECUTION

Notes

INTRODUCTION
1 cf a brief, elegant essay on the art of caricature by E H Gombrich and E Kris, *Caricature*, London 1940
2 *ibid*, pp 11-12
3 David Low, *Low's Autobiography*, London 1956, Los Angeles 1957
4 cf Egon Larsen, *Wit as Weapon, The Political Joke in History*, London 1980, pp 40ff
5 Joachim Fest, *Hitler*, London and New York 1974, p 95

YOUNG HITLER: THE MAKING OF A FAMOUS MONSTER
1 Joachim Fest, *Hitler,* p 28
2 Joachim Fest, *The Face of the Third Reich*, New York 1977, London 1979, p 34

THE NAZI MOVEMENT
1 Joachim Fest, *Hitler*, p 147
2 George Grosz, *Ade Witboi*, Berlin 1965
3 Roland Marz (ed) *John Heartfield, Der Schnitt entlang der Zeit*, Dresden 1981, p 29

THE DESTRUCTION OF THE WEIMAR REPUBLIC
1 Joachim Fest, *Hitler,* p 275
2 *ibid,* p 311
3 Oswald Spengler, *Zusammenbruch des Reiches*, quoted in *Der Deutsche in seiner Karikatur,* Stuttgart 1964, p 64

THE LEADERS OF THE NEW GERMANY
1 Joachim Fest, *Hitler*, p 456
2 H Heiber (ed) *Das Tagebuch von Joseph Goebbels 1925/26*, Stuttgart 1960, p 60

THE THOUSAND YEAR REICH
1 *Roter Aufbau*, October 1930
2 Wilhelm Reich, *The Mass Psychology of Fascism*, third English edition, New York 1970, p 80

MATTERS OF WAR AND PEACE
1 David Low, *Low's Autobiography*, London 1956, p 97
2 Raoul de Roussy de Sales (ed), A Hitler, *My New Order*, New York 1973 (reprint), p 913
3 Max Domarus, *Hitler: Reden und Proklamationen, 1932-45*, Würzburg, 1962-3, p 974
4 David Low, *op. cit*, p 249
5 *ibid*, p 250

WAR: THE ULTIMAGE GOAL
1 David Low, *Jesters in Earnest*, London 1944, preface
2 cf Joachim Fest, *Hitler*, p 612
3 Quoted in Robert Cecil (ed) *Hitler's War Machine*, London 1975, p 112
4 Z A B Zeman, *Nazi Propaganda*, second edition, London and New York 1973, pp 157-8
5 Joachim Fest, *Hitler*, p 655

Index

Numbers in italics refer to
illustrations and captions

*Adolf and August — the Munich
   Circus 20*
*Adolf, the Superman, Swallows
   Gold and Talks Crap* (Heartfield)
   71; *68*
After Ten Years: Fathers and Sons
   (Heartfield) 37; *39*
AIZ (Arbeiter-Illustrierte-Zeitung)
   37, 38, 70
Die Aktion 23
All Blown Up and Nowhere to Go
   (Low) *21*
Alt, Rudolf von 18
*Anvil Weddings Are More
   Romantic* (Low) *88*
Archimboldo 8
Arnold, Karl 18, 29, 33, 36, 37, 42,
   47, 50, 83; *22, 29, 31, 36-7, 42,
   49, 50, 51, 52*
*Art Has Become Very
   Spontaneous and Sincere
   Under the Supervision of
   National Socialism* (Roth) *72*
An Aryan is . . . 68
Aufruf 70

Barbusse, Henri 71
Barlons Vrançais (Iribe) *43*
Basic Winstonese (Low), 117, *118*
The Beast is Unleashed (Veber)
   11
Beck, Polish Minister of Foreign
   Affairs 101
The Beer Drinker 19

The Beggar's Opera (Vicky) *120*
*Beginning of the End—A
   German Hero's Death* (Godal)
   57
Belgium Revisited (Low) *110*
Berg, Alban 17
The Berlin Gang (Efimov) *56*
Berliner Lokalanzeiger 67
Berliner Tageblatt 23
Berryman, Clifford *98*
Bert 62; *13, 14-15, 63*
The Best-Seller (Raven-Hill) *42*
*The Beautiful Picture that
   Stresemann Brought from
   Munich* (Heubner) *18*
Bidlo, František 50, 59, 62, 93; *14,
   22, 52, 58, 62*
The Blood Test (Godal) 74; *69*
Blum, Léon *90*
Block, Field-Marshal von 109
Book Burning (Gerstenberg) *34*
Boris of Bulgaria *109*
Bosch, Hieronymus 33
The Boss on His Travels (Arnold)
   50
*A Breakdown: A Pleasing
   Phenomenon* (Garvens) 47; *44*
Die Brennessel 34, *79*
Breughel the Elder, Pieter 7, 8
Britische Bilder (Weber) 32
Brüning, Chancellor 47
Budapest (Whitelaw) *63*
Bulletin, Sydney *121*
The Burden of the Swastika (Low)
   40
Busch, Wilhelm 10
But We Thought If We Gave You

Teeth You'd Never Chew Us Up
   (Cummings) *104*

Can He Keep It Up? 74
*Can You Prove You Had an Aryan
   Grandmother?* (Godal) *76*
Can't We Be Friends? (Zec) *65*
Čapek, Josef 13, 71, 74; *45, 53*
La Caricature 9
Carracci, Annibale 7-8
Cause and Effect (Low) *91*
Chamberlain, Neville 97, 101; *94*
The Changing Face of Britain
   (Fougasse) 108; *107*
Le Charivari 9; *8*
The Chess Game Begins (Godal)
   85; *91*
Chicago Daily News 10; *69, 75,
   101*
Church Times 97
Churchill, Winston 105, 112, 117;
   118
*Communist and Nazi Working
   Classes* 30
Communists Fall and Shares Rise
   (Grosz) *12*
*Competition! Who is the Most
   Beautiful?* (Heartfield) 36
Consolation (Heine) *51*
The Conversion of Fritzes
   (Kukriniksy) *112*
Cross Section (Grosz) *13*
Cummings *104*
*Custodian of the 'New Order' in
   Europe* (Efimov) 113; *63*

Daladier, Edouard 101; *70, 94*

The Dance of Death 7
Danger of the Munich Beer Cellar
  (Garvens) 23
Daumier, Honoré 9, 11; 8
The Dawn (Weber) 33
Dead Men Tell No Tales (Vicky) 65
Decline of the West?
  (Gulbransson) 93
Defender of Paris (Pann) 9
The Defunct Parliament
  (Heartfield) 46
Departure from Paris (Kukriniksy)
  122
The Devils' Revolt (Godal) 61
A Dictator's Boot (Čapek), 74
Dinner of the Poor (Breughel) 8
Dinner of the Rich (Breughel) 8
Doba 74
Dobhenysk, H 68
Dolfuss, Chancellor Engelbert 85
Dollinger 79
Doré, Gustave 9
The Dove (Georges) 75; 80
Dreaming France (Iribe) 86
Das Dritte Reich in der Karikatur
  70, 74; 71
Drumming to Moscow
  (Kukriniksy) 114
Dyson, Willy 19

Ebert, Friedrich 28
Ecce Homo (Grosz) 22; 12
Eden, Sir Anthony 90
Effel, Jean 100
Efimov, Boris 15, 100, 112, 113;
  56, 63, 112
Das Einkopfgericht (Bert) 15
Einstein, Albert 34, 79
Elkins 74; 72
Ente 28; 31
Epp, Colonel von 55
Ergenbeck, Fritz 70
Ethiopia Menaces Italy (Novak)
  88; 84
Executors of the Last Will (Arnold)
  29

The Face of the Ruling Class
  (Grosz) 22
Faithful Nibelungs (Bert) 14-15
Family Group (Roth) 109
The Farce of Bayreuth 96
Fascist Lie Gun (Kukriniksy) 59
The Fate (Weber) 29; 32
Feuerbach, Anselm 18
Fitzpatrick, David, 13, 15, 84, 89,
  101, 104, 112, 113, 116; 29, 82,
  90, 93, 95, 104, 115, 117, 123
Flatters, Josef 61
For the Increase of the German
  Race (Godal) 69
For the Fatherland — To the
  Slaughterhouse (Grosz) 24
Fougasse (Cyril Kennedy) 108;
  107
Four Horsemen (Shoemaker) 10
The Four Stages of Cruelty
  (Hogarth) 8
The Fox and the Hedgehog
  (Heartfield) 100-101; 100

Franc-Tireur (Sharpshooter) 75;
  80-81
Franco, General Francisco 23, 88
Freud, Sigmund 8
Frick, Wilhelm 45, 53
Friedländer, Eugen 27
Fries, Professor 71
Fritsch, von 96
A Frog He Would A-Wooing Go
  (Zec) 9
Fulk, 53, 59
Furor Teutonicus (Niki) 36; 36

Gallieri, General 9
Garvens, Oskar 47, 74-5; 23, 44,
  73
Gateway to Stalingrad
  (Fitzpatrick) 117
Gavarni, Paul 9
Gedye, Eric 38
Geiger, Willi, 43; 45
Gellhorn, Martha 38
'Georges' 6, 80
German Academics (Dollinger) 79
German Autumn (Heine) 122
German Churches' Truce (Godal)
  76
German Michael Ready to Do
  Battle 75; 80-81
The German Way of the Cross
  (Thessig) 48
Germania (Arnold) 51
Germany Awake! (Arnold) 50
Germany, The Tidiest Country in
  the World (Bidlo) 52
Gerstenberg, Bodo 34, 54
Giles 110
Gillray, James 8, 9
Glanznummer (Weber) 32; 33
Glorifying the Führer (Kukriniksy)
  116
Godal, Eric 74, 75, 85; 57, 61, 63,
  69, 76, 91
Goebbels, Josef 14, 51, 58, 59, 62,
  67, 84, 89, 93, 97, 100, 103, 109,
  112, 117, 120; 38, 56, 58, 59, 60,
  62, 89, 116
Goebbels and Hitler (Fulk) 59
Goebbels' Puppets (Heartfield) 89
Göring, Marshal Hermann 14, 58,
  62, 88, 89, 96, 103, 108; 13, 54,
  56, 60, 85
Gott mit uns (Grosz) 12
Goya, Francisco de 105; 92
Das Grauen (Weber) 32
Grim Reaper (Georges) 6
Grosz, George 13, 18, 22-3, 36, 38,
  79, 83, 103; 12-13, 23, 24-5, 34
Guardian 121
Guernica (Picasso) 88
Gulbransson, Olaf 33, 93
Guppler 35

Halifax, Lord 97, 101
Hanfstaengl, Ernst 67
Hanshofer, Professor 64
Harvest Moon (Low) 108; 106
He is a Writer (Grosz) 34
He Must Have Been Mad (Low) 64
He Will Gas the World with His

Phrases (Heartfield) 75; 80
Heartfield, John (né Helmut
  Herzfelde) 13, 18, 23, 36-8, 43,
  47, 70, 71, 75, 79, 88, 89, 100-101,
  112; 37-8, 46-7, 68, 78, 80, 85,
  89, 100
Heiden, Konrad 70
Heine, Heinrich 10, 71
Heine, Thomas Theodor 12, 13, 36,
  47, 51; 51, 122
Hengest 121
Herzfelde, Wieland 23, 70, 79
He's Called Hermann (Bert) 13
Hess, Rudolf 58; 56, 64-5
L'Heure 10
Himmler, Heinrich 46, 58, 62, 89,
  103, 113; 56, 63
Hindenburg, President von 37,
  46-7, 51, 88
His Majesty Adolf (Heartfield) 47;
  46
His Master's Voice (Trier) 111
Hitler — A German Fate (Weber)
  21, 66
Hitler and Stalin (Kem) 99
Hitler Cancels the Treaty of
  Versailles 26
Hitler — Ein Deutsches
  Verhängniss (Niekisch) 29; 32
Hitler Has No Use for Intellectuals
  Like Einstein (Seppla) 79
Hitler Supporter (Arnold) 36
Hitler, the National Marxist
  (Arnold) 42; 42
Hitler the Saviour (Grosz) 22; 23
Hitler's Allies (Efimov) 112
Hitler's Programme (Heartfield) 38
Hit and Muss on Their Axis (Low)
  97; 97
Hoffmeister, Adolf 15, 74, 84, 93,
  108; 87, 108
Hogarth, William 8, 11
Hold It, Boys — We're Sure
  Coming! (Hengest) 121
'Horror Chamber of Art' exhibition
  (1933) 38
Horthy, Admiral 109
Hossbach, Colonel 96
Hours of the Ghosts (Heartfield)
  37
House of Cards (Low) 122
How Much for This Lot? (Low)
  113; 119
Huebner, Fr. 18
Hugenberg, Alfred 41, 42
Hughes, Billy 121
Hurrah, the Butter is Gone
  (Heartfield) 88; 85

I Wonder! I Wonder If by Any
  Chance They Really Mean It
  This Time (Dyson) 19
If Röhm Were to Marry (Bidlo) 57
In Future the Army Will be Guided
  by My Intuitions (Low) 112; 114
In the Hofbräukeller (Weber) 21
Increasing the Nordic Race (Bidlo)
  14
The Invincible Morale of the
  People (Upton) 106

Iribe, Paul *43, 86*
The Iron Comes Back (Low) 104;
  105
*It Worked at the Reichstag — Why
  Not Here?* (Low) 97; *70*
I've Settled the Fate of Jews
  (Low), *119*
Jedermann sein eigener Fussball
  36
Jekyll and Hyde (Partridge) *102*
*The Jews are Our Guests and
  They Will be Treated
  Accordingly* (Bidlo) 62; *62*
John Bull's War Aim (Partridge) *16*

Kandinsky, Wassily 18
Kaufmann, Karl 46
Keeping the Home Fires Burning
  (Low) *95*
'Kem' *99*
The Key (Strube) *97*
Kisch, Egon Erwin 67
Kladderadatsch 47, 75; *79*
Klee, Paul 18
Klimt, Gustav 17
Koch, Dr 71
Kokoschka, Oskar 17, 18
Krokodil 112
The Krupp Baby Bottle (Sennep)
  85
Krylov, Porfiri *see* Kukriniksy
Kukriniksy 116, 117; *59, 112, 114,
  116, 117, 122*
Kulturbolschewismus exhibition
  (1933) 38
Kuprianov, Mikhail *see* Kukriniksy

Langen, Albert, 12
The Last Dance 8
Laval, Pierre 108; *8, 9, 108, 109,
  119*
Lebensraum (Pelc) *92*
Le Corbusier 27
Leonardo da Vinci 8
Leopold, Hermann 70
Let Us Build Monuments (Arnold)
  47; *52*
Leviathan (Weber) 32
Ley *56, 119*
Lidové Noviny 71
Lissauer, Ernst 36
*Little Adolf Tries on the Spiked
  Moustaches* (Low) *44*
Litvinov, Maxim 101
Loos, Adolf 18, 27
Low, David 9, 13, 15, 43, 50, 58, 67,
  83-4, 88, 96-7, 100, 101, 103,
  104, 108, 110, 112-13, 117, 122;
  *21, 40, 44, 60, 64, 70, 88, 90, 91,
  94, 95, 97, 98, 99, 101, 105, 106,
  113, 114, 118-19, 122*
Ludendorff, General 19
Lush, John 9

Mahler, Gustav 17
Malik Verlag 70, 79
Mánes exhibition, Prague 38, 71,
  74, 78, 79, 93
Mann, Heinrich 70-71
Mann, Thomas 10, 70; *34*

Mannerheim, Marshal *109*
Marc, Franz 18
Mardi-Gras 108
Marxen, Herbert *31*
Masaryk, Thomas 70
The Mask 108
The Meaning of the Hitler Greeting
  (Heartfield) 43
Mein Kampf (Hitler) 28, 41; *42, 43*
Melancholia (Pelc) *111*
*Memorial to the 'Sculptor of
  Germany'* (Garvens) 74-5; *73*
Michael (Bidlo) 58
Michaelis, C and V, 70
Military Service (Grosz) *24*
Millions Stand Behind Me
  (Heartfield) *47*
Molotov, V M 101, 117
Morgenstern, Hans-Christian 10
Mottmann, Karl 18
Mrs Laval, Matchmaker
  (Hoffmeister) 108; *108*
Müller, Ludwig *74*
Mussolini, Benito 23, 83, 85, 88,
  89, 100, 109; *70, 84, 90, 91, 93,
  94, 109, 111*
Mythical Hero (Roth) 20

The Nation 75; *6, 80*
National Socialists and Capitalists
  48
Nazi Propaganda (Ente) 28; *31*
Nebelspalter 26
Die Neue Jugend (Grosz) 23
Die Neue Weltbühne 70
The New Christianity, See? (Zec) *77*
The New Reichstag . . . (Schilling)
  28
New Ruler of the World
  (Fitzpatrick) *104*
News Chronicle 117; *65, 104*
Niekisch, Ernst 29, 32
Niemöller, Pastor 92
Night of the Long Knives (Flatters)
  61
Niki, Paul 36; *36*
Nomination for 1938 (Werner) *94*
Non-Intervention Poker (Low) *90*
Novak, Josef *84*
*Now Let the Degenerate
  Democracies Show . . .* (Čapek)
  74

Old Iron . . . Old Lumber (Roth) *56*
'One Man's War Against Hitler'
  exhibition, London (1939) 38
Ordensburgen 92-3

Pacifist Hitler 75; *81*
Pann, Abel *9*
Papen, Franz von 47, 50, 51
Partridge, Bernard 9; *16, 102*
Paulus, Marshal Friedrich von 116
Peace, An Idyll (Daumier) *8*
Pelc, Antonín 84, 88, 93; *90, 92,
  93, 111*
Phillipon, Charles 9
Picasso, Pablo 88; *90*
A Piece Missing, Tovarish (Low)
  101; *101*

Pillars of Society (Grosz) *25*
Die Pleite 37; *24*
*Poland — Lebensraum for the
  Conquered* (Low) *99*
Popular Enthusiasm (Fulk) *53*
Prager Tagblatt 70
Principles of German Education
  (Čapek) *45*
*Principles of Nazi Education,
  Part II* (Čapek) *53*
Punch 9; *16, 42, 102, 107*
A Pure-Blooded Aryan
  (Dobhenysk) *68*

Quisling, Vidkun *109*

The Race Person (Arnold) *33*
Radek, Karl 78
Raeder, Admiral 96
Rake's Progress (Hogarth) 8
Raven-Hill, L *42*
Reich, Wilhelm 78-9
Reichtum aus Tränen (Weber) *32*
Reinhardt, Max 79
Rendezvous (Low) *98*
Reportage (Marxen) *31*
The Result (Godal) *63*
*Revenge — Following the
  Kaiser* 88
Ribbentrop, Joachim von *56*
Le Rire 74; *72*
Rode, Walther 70
Röhm, Ernst 55, 58-9, 62; *14-15,
  57, 61*
Roosevelt, Franklin Delano 117
Rosenberg, Alfred *56*
Roth, Stephen *20, 56, 72, 109*
Rothermere, Lord 83
Round the Clock (Whitelaw) 120;
  121
Rowlandson, Thomas 9
Russian Treachery (Low) *113*

Saar Plebiscite (Strube) *87*
The Saar Question (Hoffmeister)
  87
Salomon, Franz Pfeffer von 55, 58
*The Salon of the Dependents Has
  Achieved a Great Success*
  (Elkins) 74; *72*
Schiele, Egon 17
Schiller, Friedrich 10
Schilling, E *28*
Schirach, Baldur von 46
Schoenberg, Arnold *34*
Das Schwarze Korps 67
Sennep, J *85*
Señorita Franco (Pelc) 88; *93*
Shirer, William 78, 79
Seppla (Josef Plank) *79*
Shoemaker, Vaughn 10, 69, 75,
  101
Signac, Paul 71
Silone, Ignazio 70
Simon, Sir John 70
Simplicissimus 12, 18, 33, 36, 42,
  50, 51, 71, 93; *20, 30, 42, 50, 51,
  52*
Simplicus 70
Single-Dish Meal (Bert) *14-15*

Six Million Nazi Voters: Food for a
    Big Mouth (Heartfield) 43
Society Item (Fitzpatrick) 115
Sokolov, Nikolai see Kukriniksy
El Sol 75
Somin, W O 70
SOS German Nationalists (Arnold)
    49
The Source (Fitzpatrick) 29
Spectators at the Ringside
    (Fitzpatrick) 90
Spengler, Oswald 28, 50
Stalin, Josef 100, 101, 105, 116;
    90, 94, 98-9, 114
Stalingrad (Kukriniksy) 117
Star Turn (Weber) 32; 33
Start 1932 (Guppler) 35
Starting the Fireworks
    (Shoemaker) 75
Strasser, Gregor, 41, 42, 59
Strasser, Otto 43, 59
Streicher, Julius 62, 70; 63
Streicher (Bert) 63
Stresemann, Gustav 18
Strube, Bert 60, 87, 97
Suffer the Little Children to
    Come unto Me! (Geiger) 43; 45
Der Stürmer 62, 67; 63
Supreme Obscurantist (Efimov) 56
Surveying Europe (Fitzpatrick) 93
Swastikas (Bidlo) 22

Take Me to Czechoslovakia
    (Shoemaker) 101
Tat gegen Tinte (Hanfstaengl) 67
Teige, Karel 74
Le Témoin 86

There is a Cliff on the Volga
    (Kukriniksy) 116
Thessig, Paul 50; 48
They Salute With Both Hands Now
    (Low) 60
They Twist and Turn and Call
    Themselves German Judges
    (Heartfield) 78
This is the House That Diplomacy
    Built (Fitzpatrick) 84; 82
This Time He Left Me His Umbrella
    (Effel) 100
Through Light into Night
    (Heartfield) 38
Tiso (Slovak) 109
Toller, Ernst 67
Tretiakov, Sergei 38
Trier 111
Tucholsky, Kurt 38, 43, 97

Upper Middle-Class Nazi Types
    (Arnold) 37
Upton, Clive 106

Valentin, Karl 33
Veber, Jean 11
Very Much Alive! (Zec) 115
Vicky 117; 65, 120
Völkischer Beobachter 27
Volks-Illustrierte 37
Vorwärts 43; 48
Vot You Mean — You Think You
    Don't Know Nodding About It!
    (Giles) 110

Wagner, Richard 17
Die Wahrheit 70

War of the Germans in Uniform
    (Arnold) 31
Weber, Paul 13, 18, 28–9, 32–3, 36,
    83, 84, 116; 21, 32-3, 66
Webern, Anton von 17
Weill, Kurt 34
Weiskopf, Franz Carl 70
Wells, H G 97
Werner, Charles G 94
What News From The Second
    Front? (Low) 117; 118
What Next? (Fitzpatrick) 101, 104;
    95
What, No Chair for Me? (Low) 94
White General (Grosz) 24
Whitelaw, George 120; 63, 121
Widerstand (Resistance) 32
Will the Audience Kindly Keep
    Their Seats (Strube) 60
Wishful Thinking (Arnold) 22
Witching Hour (Heartfield) 32
Witnesses for the Prosecution
    (Fitzpatrick) 123
Wonder How Long the
    Honeymoon Will Last?
    (Berryman) 98

Yes Sir! We're All Aryans
    (Shoemaker) 69
You Will Laugh — I Know Nothing
    About it (Gerstenberg) 54

Zec, Philip, 9; 65, 77, 115

Acknowledgments

The author and publisher are grateful to the following
for supplying illustrations:

Archiv Gerstenberg, Wietz; Karl Arnold Estate,
Munich; Associated Newspapers Group Ltd, London;
Centre for the Study of Cartoons and Caricature,
University of Kent at Canterbury; Harry A Chesler
Collection, Fairleigh Dickinson University, Madison,
NJ; Falken Verlag GmbH, Niedernhausen; Galerie
Nierendorf, Berlin; The Goethe Institute, London;
Estate of George Grosz, Princeton, NJ; Gertrud
Heartfield, East Berlin; Imperial War Museum, London;
Institut Français du Royaume-Uni, London; The
Library of Congress, Washington, DC; London
Express News and Feature Services, London;
Museum of Fine Arts, Boston (W G Russell Allen
Fund); Soviet Weekly/Novosti Press Agency, London;
Syndication International, London; A Paul Weber
Estate, Ratzeburg; The Wiener Library, London.